Self-Esteem Revolutions in Children

Understanding and Managing the Critical Transitions in Your Child's Life

SELF-ESTEEM
Revolutions
IN CHILDREN

Thomas W. Phelan, Ph.D.

CHILD MANAGEMENT INC

Glen Ellyn, Illinois

Illustrations by Margaret Mayer
Cover copy by Brett Jay Markel
Child Management Logo by Steve Roe

Distributed by LPC Group, Login Trade Division

Printed in the United States of America
10 9 8 7 6 5 4 3 2 1

For more information, contact:
Child Management, Inc.
800 Roosevelt Road
Glen Ellyn, Illinois 60137

Publisher's Cataloging in Publication
(Prepared by Quality Books Inc.)

Phelan, Thomas W., 1943-
    Self-esteem revolutions in children / Thomas W. Phelan.
    p. cm.
    Includes bibliographical references.
    ISBN: 1-889140-01-5

1. Self-esteem in children. 2. Parent and child.   I. Title.

BF723.S3P44 1996   155.4
                                      QBI96-40224

To the many children
who over twenty-five years
have taught me a lot about self-esteem

Contents

Preface

After all that has been written about raising children, do we know today what it takes to be a good parent? I think we do. It's certainly easier said than done, but good parents provide for two essential qualities in their children: *self-discipline and self-esteem.*

Providing for a child's self-discipline means having reasonable, effective and non-abusive strategies for (1) controlling obnoxious behavior (e.g., arguing, whining, fighting) and (2) encouraging good behavior (e.g., eating, going to bed, doing homework, getting along with others). Parents who are good disciplinarians know how to set limits. They can say "No" to their children and stick to it without being manipulated to death by tantrums, threats or badgering. They also expect something of their children. They are "demanding" in the most constructive sense of the word, and their long-term goal is for their own discipline to become their child's self-discipline.

Providing good discipline, however, is only half the job. Parents must also do things that help children to feel accepted and to realistically believe in themselves. We want our children to feel they are lovable and competent. We want them to be able to enjoy other people and to believe that they themselves can muster the courage and effort necessary to handle life's challenges. This is the essence of self-esteem, and promoting this requires—in addition to discipline—listening, affection, praise, shared fun and parental self-control. It requires a practical commitment to caring for the physical and emotional needs of a child.

It also requires that parents have a down-to-earth understanding of self-esteem. They need to realize that children's self-esteem undergoes sweeping revolutions as youngsters grow up. Self-esteem may start out as simply a love-based matter, but soon enough it also becomes rooted in competence. And it steadily becomes more and more complicated, as later years add the dimensions of character, academic performance, relationships with friends, romantic appeal and career choice. The child's job is not an easy one.

Authoritarian vs. Permissive Parenting

The notion that both discipline and parental warmth and acceptance are essential to decent self-respect was clearly stated in Coopersmith's landmark 1967 research, *Antecedents of Self-Esteem*. At about the same time these ideas were further clarified in another important series of studies by Diana Baumrind. As she pointed out, promoting the self-discipline and self-esteem of one's children often requires an emotional juggling act by parents—as well as by teachers and other caregivers. It is not easy to be firm and demanding one minute, then warm and affectionate the next. Some adults naturally have personalities or temperaments that predispose them toward one or the other. Baumrind described three basic parenting styles: authoritarian, permissive and authoritative.

Parents who tend to *overemphasize* the discipline side of the equation were referred to as authoritarian. Authoritarian parents are demanding in the worst sense of the word. They are intimidators, requiring obedience and respect above all else. They become overly angry and forceful when they don't get that obedience and respect. Their love and acceptance appear totally conditional to the child. They do not listen to their kids or explain the reasons for their expectations, which are frequently unrealistic. They often see their children's individuality and independence as irrelevant or threatening.

Research has shown that authoritarian parents tend to produce children who are more withdrawn, anxious, mistrustful and discontented. These children are often overlooked by their peers. Their self-esteem is often poor.

Parents who *overemphasize* the self-esteem side of the equation were referred to as permissive. They may be warm and supportive, but they are not good disciplinarians. They make only weak demands for good behavior and they tend to avoid or ignore obnoxious behavior. They seem to believe that children should grow up without any anger, tears or frustrations. They reinforce demanding and inconsiderate behavior from their children. Their love and acceptance are "unconditional" in the worst sense of the word, for they set few limits on what their children do.

Research has shown that permissive parents tend to produce children who are more immature, demanding, and dependent. These children are often rejected by their peers. As we shall see, their self-esteem is often unrealistic and hard to interpret, for they often blame others for their misfortunes.

The Authoritative Model

Parents who are able to provide for both the discipline and self-esteem needs of their youngsters Baumrind referred to as authoritative. They clearly communicate high—but not unrealistic—demands for their children's behavior. They expect good things from their kids and reinforce those things when they occur. When kids act up, on the other hand, authoritative parents respond with firm limits, but without fits of temper. They are warm, reasonable and sensitive to a child's needs. They are supportive of a child's individuality and encourage growing independence.

Authoritative parents tend to produce competent children. These kids are more self-reliant, self-controlled and happier. They are usually accepted and well-liked by their peers. Their self-esteem is good.

Logic and research, then, support the idea that children need both discipline and self-esteem to grow up psychologically healthy. We have dealt with the discipline side of the equation elsewhere in *1-2-3 Magic: Effective Discipline for Children 2-12,* and to a large extent in its "sequel,"

Surviving Your Adolescents: How to Manage and Let Go of Your 13-18 Year Olds, which also recognizes the need to respect the growing independence of the adolescent. *Self-Esteem Revolutions in Children* is an effort to address the other side of the parenting equation. What needs to be done—and what needs to be avoided—to provide for adequate self-esteem in our children? As we shall see, good intentions are not enough. Self-esteem does not automatically fall out of the sky, nor does it drop from the mouths of well-intentioned adults.

Introduction

L et's begin with a strange question. Which is harder to do: grow up or learn to play the piano?

Certainly, learning the piano is a daunting task. First you must learn what this thing called a piano is. Then you must determine what those black and white keys are for, and discover why—every once in a while—there seems to be a black key missing between two white ones. As if that weren't bad enough, the thing is no good at all if you don't also learn something about music. You must master a seemingly unending series of mysteries: time, sharps and flats, base clef and treble clef, signatures, eighth notes and quarter notes, EGBDF and FACE.

And all this is just the beginning, because after this comes practice, practice, practice. Interminable boredom when you'd rather be outside playing with your friends. But, if you stick with it, more and more the drudgery begins to be sprinkled with a sense of accomplishment. There's nice music coming out of this thing and *I'm* doing it!

But then there are always those darned recitals. Some of those other kids are, like, really awesome! But challenge is what learning a musical instrument is all about. It's a tough going.

What about growing up? Piano is arduous, but when they think about it, most people would probably agree that growing up is harder. For one thing, it's a twenty-four-hour-a-day job, week after week, and year after year. For another thing, it involves not just one task but many, and you can't quit "taking lessons" as you can with the piano. In addition, growing up often means handling, as best you can, things that are beyond your control, such as your parents' behavior, what you look like and where you come from, how smart you are and the irritable teacher you have in fifth grade.

Growing up also involves a lot of effort, not to mention guts. No, as a matter of fact, I don't feel like going to school today, but I have to. I also want to keep those grades up. And there's a basketball game on TV tonight, but I have swimming; I've got to improve my time in the 100 meter freestyle before the next meet. I want to ask that cute girl from History class for a date, but—though I'd never admit it—the thought scares me to death. But I'll feel like a wimp if I chicken out. My self-esteem will be zero. But then again, what will it be if she says "No"?

Revolutions

Growing up and self-esteem are wedded forever. In fact, in a very real sense, self-esteem is an indicator of how well the job of growing up is going. Though adults often seem to forget it, children are evaluating themselves all the time. Kids are always keenly sensitive to how they are doing with the tasks that life hands them. They want to do well.

If it is anything, though, growing up is a revolutionary business. The job keeps changing in all kinds of fundamental ways. The "bottom line" isn't always the same. In the beginning our youngsters have to learn to walk, to stop throwing food on the floor and to go to the bathroom. Then, just when they are mastering the tasks of dressing themselves, tying their shoes and not slugging other kids when provoked, they wind up in school.

Now there are all those numbers and letters to memorize, and while they're doing this they have to sit real still for what seems like an eternity. There are also gym and music and art to conquer. On the playground they learn how to have fun with friends, and also how to stay clear of those big third-graders who, it seems, are always wanting to pick on smaller kids.

As growing up proceeds, the revolutions continue. The job keeps changing and getting more complex. New layers and dimensions are always being added. And, as growing up keeps being revolutionized, the foundations of self-esteem keep being revolutionized.

The basis of character changes from simply good behavior to good behavior plus effort, the ability to confront anxiety and concern for other people. Academic competence eventually translates into career choice and preparation. The social dimension adds loyalty to friends of the same sex and then, later, the fascinating and awkward attribute known as romantic appeal.

There are revolutions from inside as well as from outside. In the beginning self-esteem is a brief and fleeting notion, based on concrete events in the here-and-now: a brief moment of pride or frustration, then it's gone. Later on, however, as a child develops the ability to remember and to think more abstractly, self-esteem becomes a more permanent resident in the youngster's mental space. Indeed, a favorite pastime of adolescents, fortunately or unfortunately, is evaluating themselves during moments of quiet when nothing much else is going on.

Almost all children must deal with the most basic self-esteem revolutions: the transition from self-esteem based on the "unconditional" love of parents to self-esteem based on one's own *competence* and on the *conditional love* of other people. Many children must also manage idiosyncratic self-esteem revolutions, based on events such as divorce, geographical moves, drastic changes in physical appearance at adolescence, the loss of—or beginning of—a romantic relationship, or the onset of anxiety or depression.

Growing up is a changing, challenging and exciting business. Self-esteem, which is forever entangled with it, has its ups and downs, its intricacies and its mysteries.

The funny thing is, however, that some adults treat the acquisition of self-esteem as if it were easier than learning to play the piano. They ignore, in other words, the self-esteem revolutions in children. This is an injustice to children and a gross oversimplification of the task of growing up.

Self-Esteem Revolutions in Children will help adults bring the issue of self-esteem back to reality. To be effective in assisting their children with this challenge, parents must first understand the self-esteem revolutions (Chapters 1-10). Then they must be able to help their children manage and survive them (Chapters 11-18).

The best musician in the world can't confer immediate Carnegie Hall status on an aspiring pianist. Way back in grammar school we were taught that during the process of hatching, the baby chick needs to break its own shell and climb out on its own. If it doesn't, its strength can be impaired permanently. In the same way, our children need to develop their strength —physically and mentally—by conquering challenges and overcoming their own failures as they grow up. Parents can help, but they should never try to take this job away from their children—or pretend it isn't there.

As a parent you cannot bestow instant self-esteem on your children. What you can do, however, is help them earn it.

Part I

The Self-Esteem
Puzzle

Brain Twister

No one is indifferent to the role self-esteem plays in his or her life. Put ego on the line, and people are passionately involved right off the bat. It's a bad hair day, and Margie is crushed every time she thinks people are looking at her funny in the halls. After a week of suspense, Emily is on cloud nine when she receives an A on her marine biology paper. Richard is devastated for days after he fumbles the ball on the 2-yard line.

Self-esteem is a strange phenomenon. It pops up where one wouldn't expect, often in odd and seemingly trivial ways. Is it self-esteem, for example, that is behind the aggressive antics of the usual road maniac? Matt gets irritated and speeds up while some guy is trying to pass him on the tollway. He then lays on the horn when the person pulls back in front of him a little too closely. No one is going to get ahead of him or cut him off without hearing about it!

What about the fanatical loyalty of many professional sports fans? Why is Dad so crabby after "his" football team loses the game 17-16 on a field goal in the last minute? "I can't believe *we* blew it in the last 43 seconds!" he moans. Did he go to high school with these guys—or isn't it true that he's never met any of them? Could it be his ego is bound up with a bunch of people with whom he has nothing in common but the name of a city?

Not all manifestations of the urge for self-esteem, however, are trivial or odd. The search for self-esteem, for example, may play a role in the more than one million pregnancies that occur every year in single teenagers. Studies have shown that—before they become pregnant—many of these young girls have a poor image of themselves. Since at their age the dimension of romantic appeal, which includes physical attractiveness and social acceptance, is extremely important, these girls are vulnerable. Sex can easily be felt as a wonderful—though temporary—"self-esteem hit" that seems to confirm their attractiveness and personal value.

The importance that people attribute to self-regard has hit an amazing level in the past few decades. We have become consumers of large numbers of books on the subject. Some of these instruct parents how to nurture self-esteem in their children, and others are intended to help the kids themselves develop some sense of self-respect. Self-esteem is described as "a basic need for every human being" and "our most important psychological resource."

Educators—and even the whole State of California—have also come to endorse the "bottom line" importance of self-esteem. One teacher's manual, used in a school self-esteem program, declares that "every child deserves to believe that she or he is truly a wonder" and that "nothing is as important as self-esteem to a child's well-being and success." Self-esteem programs in the schools have multiplied rapidly throughout the country.

When one researches the notion of self-esteem, several interesting problems pop up right at the start. First, the notion of self-esteem itself is confusing. People talk about it as if it were a separate entity inside a person, but at the same time it seems to be intertwined with almost every aspect of an individual's life. Adding to the quandary, it appears that people with good self-esteem are usually competent and successful, but it is also obvious that, not infrequently, some competent and successful people—children and adults—don't think much of themselves. In fact, for some of these people it appears that poor self-esteem makes them more likeable as well as more motivated!

Second, there appears to be an almost religious quality to much of the writing about self-esteem. However fuzzy, shifting and ethereal the notion of self-esteem might be, everyone seems to agree that self-esteem should be treated as a sacred object. Trying to discover and describe the actual "nuts-and-bolts" of self-esteem begins to feel like some kind of sacrilegious act. Brutal honesty is prohibited once you enter the inner sanctum.

Cause or Effect?

Nevertheless, enthusiasm for efforts to enhance or protect the self-respect of children draws some support from research. Studies have consistently shown that various levels of self-esteem correspond with certain personal characteristics. People who have good to high self-esteem, for example, tend to show the following qualities:

1. They are more often in a better mood and their moods don't fluctuate much.
2. They are more outgoing and comfortable with other people. They feel good about—and look forward to—meeting new people because they expect to be liked and accepted.
3. They are more confident, optimistic and willing to try new things. They anticipate most new challenges with enthusiasm and excitement.
4. They are persistent during a task. They have "HFT"—high frustration tolerance. They can put up with minor—or even greater—annoyances or roadblocks because they expect to succeed sooner or later.
5. They are healthier, both physically and mentally.
6. They are able to operate independently and show both initiative and responsiblity in their actions.
7. They take a realistic amount of credit for and feel good about their accomplishments.

On the other hand, people with poor self-esteem tend to operate—as expected—in opposite ways:

1. They tend to be more anxious, irritable and depressed. Their mood is more negative and changeable, and often they also manifest psychosomatic symptoms (e.g. headaches) as well.
2. They are more self-conscious and less comfortable around others because they fear they will not be liked. They are often quieter because they are afraid of saying something stupid.
3. They anticipate new challenges with fear, because they are worried they will not be up to the task, and that disaster or embarrassment will result.
4. They give up more quickly during a task. They have "LFT"—low frustration tolerance. Minor frustrations simply remind them of past failures, and they are not optimistic about resolving difficulties on their own.
5. They are more vulnerable to health problems, as evidenced by the link between poor self-esteem and problems such as drug abuse, unwanted pregnancy and eating disorders.
6. They are more easily influenced by others because of their need to be liked, and thus more apt to do things that they really aren't proud of.
7. They tend to remember vividly their failures, but have trouble taking credit for their legitimate successes. When successful, they see themselves as "imposters" who have somehow just lucked out.

At first glance, these correlations appear to be powerful evidence that supports any attempt to improve the self-esteem of youngsters. Improve self-esteem and you should improve everything else.

One day, however, a humorless skeptic came along who asked an interesting question: "What's causing what here? Is a person's success caused by her high self-esteem, or is her self-esteem the result of her success?"

Does it work like this?

SELF-ESTEEM > SUCCESS

Many people thought it did. One was a well-known psychologist and researcher, Albert Bandura. In a 1977 article he wrote, "Not only can perceived self-efficacy have directive influence on choice of activities and settings, but, through expectations of eventual success, it can affect the coping efforts once they are initiated.... The stronger the perceived self-efficacy, the more active the efforts." What Bandura was trying to say, in plain English, is that people with higher self-esteem will try harder because they expect to succeed. People with lower self-esteem will give up sooner. And trying harder, of course, will more often produce success.

That seems logical enough, but so does the alternative. Perhaps self-esteem is the effect of success rather than the cause. In other words, it might work like this:

SUCCESS > SELF-ESTEEM

Supporting this point of view is another psychologist, Martin Seligman. In *What You Can Change... And What You Can't*, he wrote, "Low self-esteem is an *epiphenomenon*, a mere reflection that your commerce with the world is going badly. It has no power in itself. What needs improving is not self-esteem but your commerce with the world." In other words, if your self-esteem is poor, it's because something is going wrong in your life.

In questioning the "hype" about self-esteem, the wet blanket contingent draws further support from several other facts. First of all, although many research studies demonstrate a correlation between self-esteem and achievement, the correlations are consistently quite low. This means that many other things are also responsible for achievement—perhaps things like ability, effort and parental involvement. Second, there has been no evidence that self-esteem programs do, in fact, raise self-esteem or that they produce any other tangible benefits. Third, there is no evidence that a majority of our children have a problem with their self-esteem in the first place. As a matter of fact, as we shall see, the self-esteem of very young children is usually unrealistically high.

The question, cause or effect, is still not an easy one to answer, but it is a legitimate one. If one's self-respect is, in fact, caused by his somehow being healthier, less moody, more persistent and more comfortable with other people in the first place, then our time, money and effort to raise self-esteem might be better spent working directly on improving things like our children's health, moods, effort and interpersonal skills.

Complicating the self-esteem picture are other questions. If doing well produces self-respect, how can it be that one of the most common problems psychologists and psychiatrists deal with is people who are competent and well-liked but have low self-esteem? On the other hand, if high self-esteem produces success, how is it that in many people low self-esteem gives them a powerful drive that makes them very successful?

What is self-esteem based on? Is it love? Success? Acclaim? Or can adequate self-respect be rooted in the simple fact that a person is a human being? And who is the final judge of an individual's goodness or worth? Do parents hand a child a self-image, or does the child have something to say about it?

2

Speculation About Self-Esteem

S elf-esteem is more puzzling than people often realize. In trying to unravel its nature, over the years a number of psychological authorities have proposed different theories, coming at the problem from very different angles. Most of these authorities see self-esteem as a feeling that results when people evaluate themselves or their behavior—when they appraise, in other words, their self-concept or a part of it. Writers and researchers disagree, however, when it comes to both the basis of self-esteem—what people evaluate about themselves, and who, ultimately, is doing the judging.

The Basis of Self-Esteem

Is self-esteem based on accomplishment or success? One of the earliest— and perhaps one of the more honest—writers on the subject, William James, believed that self-esteem depends on how competent a person is in the tasks he chooses as important to himself—or what they "backed themselves to be." If I have "staked my all on being a psychologist," he said in 1890 in *Principles of Psychology*, then that's where my self-esteem is going to live or die. For most adults, James pointed out, how well they do in their chosen line of work has a great impact on their feeling of self-worth. Children today, on the other hand, have no choice but to "stake their all," in a sense, on their full-time job, school. This daily task, according to James' theory, should have a large effect on how they feel about themselves. Feeling competent at the important tasks of one's life makes for good self-esteem.

Not so, said another well-known author, George Herbert Mead. The real deal has to do with relationships with other people. In *Mind, Self, and Society*, written in 1934, he proposed that self-esteem is basically an interpersonal phenomenon. To him self-esteem depends upon one's sense of belonging—how well you are accepted by the important people in your life. This does not mean just superficially "getting along" with others; it also includes your ability to have close, honest and emotionally satisfying relationships as well. According to Mead, man is primarily a social animal, and people feel good about themselves when they have satisfying and enduring relationships with family, friends, and acquaintances, and feel they are contributing to society at large.

None of the above, say other experts: the true bottom line is having a sense that you are in control of your life. In an article entitled "Human Autonomy: The Basis for True Self-Esteem," Edward Deci and Richard Ryan claim that "true self-esteem" is based on the amount of self-determination a person realizes in her life. From this point of view what is really important is an individual's perception that her inherent, unique potential is being realized through her own efforts.

Hold the phone, suggests another interesting line of thought. Success, relationships with others and feeling you are in control of your life are all things that can let you down. You can't always count on them. You can, however, count on yourself. In their book, *Self-Esteem: Paradoxes and Innovations in Clinical Theory and Practice,* Richard Bednar and Scott Peterson argue that the real bottom line for self-esteem is your effort to *cope* with life—no matter how things turn out. According to them, people really feel good about themselves when they see themselves as facing problems and their associated anxieties rather than avoiding them. You are proud of yourself, in other words, for having guts and for trying, *regardless of the outcome of your efforts*. All that you can ask, they say, is that you face facts and try your best, because you can't always control the results. How you wage the war itself is what is important. What determines your level of self-esteem is the amount of courage you show and the amout of effort you put forth.

Not so fast, say Mssrs. E. Markus and H. Wurf. What's all this talk about "global," one-dimensional self-esteem in the first place? In an article entitled "The dynamic self-concept: a social psychological perspective," they say that a problem with these other theories is the perception of self-esteem as a unitary thing. In reality, they say, it may have different parts that depend on both internal motives as well as on the different situations people find themselves in. William James had also recognized that self-esteem might vary depending on someone's immediate circumstances. In other words, there might be a kind of overall, global self-esteem, but there may also be specific "self-esteems" that occur when people evaluate themselves in particular situations. Children, for example, might have an "academic self-esteem" and a "social self-esteem."

Implied in most of the ideas mentioned so far is the notion that *self-esteem is a product of something else*, such as success, positive personal relationships, courage or effort. As you may have already guessed, though, this fundamental notion doesn't sit well with everyone, either. There is room for a more radical viewpoint.

Psychotherapists to the Rescue

A psychotherapist's job is to help people feel better. Clients come to the office suffering from anxiety, depression, guilt or anger. They often feel their lives are a mess. The important thing is to help them to feel better, whatever it takes.

A number of psychotherapists, feeling compassion for the self-esteem-related pain of their patients, began writing about the problem of self-esteem. It was probably only a matter of time until they got around to the ultimate prescription for what to evaluate about yourself: *nothing!* In *A New Guide to Rational Living*, Ellis and Harper suggest that if you only feel bad when you are rating or judging yourself on one of life's tasks or dimensions, you obviously shouldn't rate yourself on your success or behavior in the first place. From their perspective, any internal judge is nothing but a big troublemaker. What good does it do to be appraising yourself all the time, and how can you really evaluate your "whole self" anyway? Just knock it off. You should feel worthwhile simply because you're a human being—which beats being a frog by a long shot—and you still exist.

Matthew McKay, in *Self-Esteem*, expresses a similar sentiment. "Every criterion ever devised for measuring human worth," he writes, "is dependent on its cultural context." Therefore all these standards are simply arbitrary, useless and troublesome. One solution to the self-esteem problem, he suggests, is to admit that true human worth is impossible to determine. Or, he says, look at it another way. If human worth does exist, why not see it as equally distributed and unchangeable? Everyone gets one unit of worth at birth which is "absolutely equal to everyone else's unit of worth." Not only that, "no matter what happens in your life, no matter what you do or is done to you, your human worth can't be diminished or increased." What a relief that would be.

Who Is Doing the Judging

Other authorities explored a different aspect of the problem: when it comes to self-esteem, who is the final judge? There are obviously two contestants for the job: the individual himself and other people.

Many authors suggest that a person's self-image depends on how he incorporates the feedback about himself that he receives from others. Perhaps the most well-known of these theorists is Charles Cooley, who in 1902 came up with the famous notion of the "looking glass self."

As they grow up, Cooley says, children's self-concept and subsequent self-esteem develop from the opinions (verbal and nonverbal) of significant other people, like parents and teachers. These other people are like a mirror that the inexperienced and naive child can see himself reflected in. By means of this mirror children can tell how they are doing with life's tasks. From significant other people, for example, they develop their ideas about how capable or likable they are.

Other theorists took exception to this. This isn't the way it should be. In 1983 Rollo May, in *The Discovery of Being*, argued that self-esteem ultimately depends instead on how you see yourself, rather than on feedback or ideas from the minds of other people. The opinions of others are too fragile a foundation, because they can change at any moment. What some call "inner" self-esteem (based on one's own opinion) should be more important than "outer" self-esteem (based on others' opinions). Your own opinions are what mattered most. To May, genuine self-esteem depends on having the courage to be true to yourself—to be "authentic"—and to realize your inherent potentials, even if doing this runs the risk of producing displeasure in other people.

In *Pulling Your Own Strings*, Wayne Dyer pursues a similar but slightly different theme in saying that people need to avoid the "comparison trap." You will always be anxious, he says, if "your assessments of yourself are always controlled by something outside you which you cannot possibly regulate." You need not "look outside yourself for self-assessment," he continues, because the "more important barometer for your self-measurements...is your own satisfaction with the way your life is going."

The Conclusion?

Obviously, a number of different people have forwarded a number of different theories about self-esteem. Understandably, some have given up the battle to figure it out entirely, saying that there isn't any way to sum up, or know, who or what you really are. Some theorists have tried to describe how self-esteem actually operates, while others have expressed opinions about how it *should* work. Psychotherapists, on the other hand, more often have been simply concerned with what ideas make patients feel better, regardless of their theoretical validity.

There has always been confusion and disagreement over the nature of self-esteem. That has not stopped people, however, from trying to develop methods for improving it.

3

Charging the Battery?

Many interesting approaches have been designed either to repair poor self-esteem in struggling youngsters or to enhance self-esteem in kids who were already doing pretty well. The idea, in a sense, was to locate the self-esteem part inside children, and then to do something positive or invigorating to it—sort of like charging the battery in a car or doing a tune-up on an engine.

These approaches came about for two obvious reasons. First of all, as we have just seen, people felt that good things seemed to "go along with" good self-esteem. These good things included characteristics such as confidence in the face of new challenges, lower anxiety, good health and positive interpersonal relationships. Ignoring the cause and effect question, many people saw self-esteem as a powerful internal force that could seriously impact many other aspects of an individual's life. If we can raise self-esteem, they reasoned, then naturally these other things should improve as well.

Second, not all kids were doing well in the self-esteem struggle. Parents and teachers, understandably, were extremely concerned with the idea of kids feeling badly about themselves. They'd seen the look in the eyes of the child in the frozen food aisle who was just slapped in the face in front of five other people. They'd also seen the girl on the playground who is teased because she has no father, or the overweight boy with whom no other child would be caught dead. Witnessing these mini-tragedies, adults felt horrible.

If kids were suffering from low self-regard, it was imperative to try to repair it or raise it as quickly as possible. Then everyone—adults and children—could feel better. To try to help, parents, teachers, school districts, therapists and even one whole state all got into the act. Unfortunately, in spite of the best motives, fuzzy thinking about self-esteem often produced tactics that were out of touch with reality and that did little good.

Groups for Children

Kids identified as having self-esteem problems have sometimes been involved in "self-esteem groups" conducted in the schools or by private therapists. These groups would usually meet once a week for an hour or so. The people who conducted these groups were often delightful and engaging. The goal of the group experience was to provide the participating children with some positive experiences with other children that would help them to feel better about themselves. Sometimes structured games were used to try to get across the idea to kids that—in spite of everything—they are really OK. Groups sometimes also attempted to teach children how to think differently in order to get rid of unnecessary self-criticism.

Some of these groups were fun for the children, especially if they were younger. For those who were having academic troubles, these groups sometimes provided a welcome relief from the regular classroom. For those who were having social problems, the close supervision of the group situation usually didn't allow for the kinds of negative interactions that the children often encountered on the playground, at lunch, before school or at recess. Many of the group leaders were friendly, supportive people whom the kids really liked and who gave the children lots of positive reinforcement.

How much did these self-esteem groups really change children's self-esteem? Unfortunately, not a lot, though there may have been different reasons for this for younger children (pre-junior high) than for older kids. Even when the younger children had a positive experience for one hour once a week in the group, it didn't carry over into the rest of their lives. Those with low self-esteem still had to go back to the playground where they were treated poorly every day. They also had to go back to the challenges of the classroom where they had trouble with reading and hated math. If their self-esteem problems were partly based on their family life, a group experience also did little to end the negative encounters there.

For older children, on the other hand, involvement in a self-esteem group could be quite a different story, because of a destructive paradox. Often for these adolescents and preadolescents, the very fact of being involved in a self-esteem group—in and of itself—lowered their self-esteem. They were being singled out as having a problem and they were embarrassed about it. They saw it as being identified with "a bunch of losers," and they were often mortified. When they went to their group, they felt everyone was watching them, knew where they were going (many did know) and was concluding that they too were a loser.

Classroom Programs

Elsewhere, in regular classrooms, self-esteem "exercises" were some-times conducted, without anyone having to be identified as having a problem. Different ideas would be presented, often through film or slides, and class discussion might follow. Some programs, for example, focused on the tendency of many youngsters to criticize themselves unfairly. The relationship of this kind of "self-talk" to self-concept and self-esteem was pointed out, as well as how poor self-esteem could become a "self-fulfilling prophecy," leading to unproductive and self-defeating behavior. Kids were shown how to avoid this trap by using self-affirmations rather than put-downs.

Other programs stressed how to build self-esteem, in addition to dealing with how one perceived oneself. It's time to get out there and do something, they emphasized, rather than just thinking about everything all the time. One unit, for example, taught four steps for building self-esteem. The first step was to identify one's strengths, which was often difficult for kids who were used to being self-critical. Step two was to engage in positive life experiences with positive kinds of people. This often involved a sense of risk-taking. Third, it was suggested that you try to go in small steps, rather than biting off more than you could chew at one time. Finally, after achieving something worthwhile, the youngster should savor her success and give herself a pat on the back.

Another regular class exercise was called "Fishing for Compliments." Kids were grouped into bunches of five or six students. Each was given a piece of paper and instructed to put their name at the top. The papers were then exchanged and each person was instructed to write a compliment for the person whose name appeared at the top. There were spaces on the sheet for six compliments, and next to each space was the picture of a fish. At the end of the exercise, children were asked, "How does it feel to receive so many compliments?"

In another activity the teacher asked an individual student to stand on a table. The other students were then instructed to gather around and applaud. Each student got a turn being applauded at one time or another, and at the end of the day they took home a brightly colored card that said, "I'm terrific!"

Teachers who ran these regular classroom programs had several things to say about them. They felt, for example, that the ideas about reducing self-criticism and the steps for building self-esteem were basically good ideas. The kids who could relate to these ideas were the kids who didn't really need them, because their self-esteem was already pretty good. However, the kids who were suffering from poor self-concept didn't appear to take the message out of the classroom with them.

On the other hand, things like the Fishing for Compliments and applause exercises, teachers pointed out, were too easy for kids—especially older ones—to see through. Even the phrase "fishing for compliments," for example, usually implies an insecure person urging others in subtle ways to offer praise in a manner that may or may not be justified. Kids felt embarrassed about this and didn't always know what to write as a compliment to someone they didn't really know, or worse, didn't really like. Many of their comments were neutral or bland. Even when the comments were positive, however, they tended to be dismissed because they—like the applause—were not offered spontaneously or sincerely.

California Dreaming

One of the more interesting—and controversial—approaches to the problem of self-esteem originated in the State of California. In the late 1980s a Democratic Assemblyman convinced the state's political establishment that self-esteem was a critical issue in crime, drug abuse, scholastic failure and a few other things. The result was the formation of the California Task Force to Promote Self-Esteem, which had the modest goal of improving the self-respect of everyone in the state. Three years and $735,000 later, the group issued *Toward a State of Esteem: the Final Report of the California Task Force to Promote Self-Esteem and Personal and Social Responsibility*.

The "Personal and Social Responsibility" parts were added because the original idea triggered a good deal of criticism. Unfortunately, the flaws in the original concept as well as the vague and unrealistic language of the report itself drew further attacks. *U.S. News & World Report* called the whole thing "a terrible idea" and "yet another California joke." *Fortune* magazine referred to the report as "baby talk" and "knuckleheaded chuckleworthy material." John Leo of *U.S. News* worried that the report "wanted to treat each child like a fragile therapy consumer in constant need of an ego boost," and that the report's basic philosophy was anti-competition, anti-achievement, and anti-success. This point of view, he felt, would—among other things—result in a lowering of standards in the schools and the production of less competent children.

The point of view Leo was worried about had gained momentum some years before the California Task Force on Self-Esteem ever appeared. In 1976, in a small book called *Self-Worth and School Learning*, Martin Covington and Richard Beery stated that our schools have become overly focused on evaluation. The result is that children's self-esteem has become identified with academic achievement, and constant evaluation and testing cause kids to become excessively fearful of making mistakes. In 1969 similar ideas were expressed in another influential book, *Schools without Failure*, by William Glasser.

According to these authors, part of the solution to the problem is to get rid of competition. This means, among other things, getting rid of the signs of competition, like grades and awards. Another part of the solution is to teach children to accept themselves "exactly as they are." As one well-known self-esteem manual, *Just Because I Am: A Child's Book of Affirmation*, puts it, "A child's value is unconditional. Nothing the child does, says, or chooses can change it."

The result of these philosophies in many schools is what Charles J. Sykes, in *Dumbing Down Our Kids*, calls "feel-good learning." What has become more and more emphasized, he says, are the feelings and the uniqueness of each individual. Just trying should be good enough. "Educationists," as Sykes calls them, feel that self-esteem should no longer be "the product of achievement, or hard work, or the mastery of a difficult task." They believe that children have a "right to feel good about themselves" just the way they are already.

Sykes sees many problems with this approach. To "feel-good" educators, trying is good enough. In the real world, however, it isn't. No employer is going to pay an annual salary to someone simply because she tries. In addition, kids compare themselves to their peers all the time, no matter what the adults are doing. Even without grades, students know who is doing well—and who isn't—academically as well as athletically. Perhaps most important for him, Sykes feels that the new approach runs the danger of *decreasing skills while improving self-concept*. He points to the startling and unsettling results of one study. In this study it was found that in international comparisons of math abilities American students ranked last in their *performance*. When asked, however, how they *felt* about their math abilities, they ranked first!

Lies My Parents Taught Me

Along with the hope for a quick self-esteem fix, wishful thinking and denial have also led intelligent and caring adults to offer occasional bits of encouragement to children. They have shared—or sometimes repeated ad nauseam—questionable pieces of advice or ways of looking at things that had sounded good to them in the past. Some of these bits of "collective wisdom" have more merit than others, but they not only don't do much good, they also tend to mislead youngsters about the nature of reality. Here are some of the more common ones:

1. "You're unique and special. You should feel good about yourself because there's no one else exactly like you."
2. "Don't compare yourself to other children. The only thing that matters is how you're doing, and you're only really competing against yourself."
3. "It's not whether you win or lose, it's how you play the game."
4. "Everyone is good at something and bad at something. It all evens out."
5. "If you can dream it, you can do it."
6. "Don't rate yourself on your behavior. We will love and accept you no matter what."
7. "It makes no difference what others think of you. The only thing that matters is what you think of yourself."
8. "You're wonderful just the way you are."
9. "You shouldn't judge yourself on the basis of things you can't control."

Some of these ideas are partly true, and some are totally false. All of them, however, sacrifice honesty in an altruistic attempt to make someone else feel better. On the other hand, they are only ideas, and any harm they may cause is limited by the fact that kids don't easily take any idea with them to the classroom, to the playground or to the street.

Oversimplified and Off-Target

In spite of the sincere compassion and commendable motives behind some of these approaches to the problem of self-esteem, they haven't changed things very much. Some may have had a short-term impact on self-esteem. The best may have—like an aspirin—provided temporary relief from pain, while the worst actually ran the risk of further damaging a child's self-concept.

There are several reasons why we can't point to any concrete evidence that these efforts to raise self-esteem do, in fact, accomplish this goal. First, some of the programs or activities mentioned above are so brief that they can't have much impact. One hour per week by itself is rarely going to revolutionize what any child thinks of himself. He still has to deal with the real world that created the problem in the first place—and continues to reinforce it. Overnight summer camp experiences, for example, often provide some of the most refreshing and potent breaks from poor self-esteem, especially for children with major school or family problems. Camps have the advantage of providing a totally different environment for a concentrated (24 hours a day) and fairly lengthy (two months or so) period of time. No school, no family. The difficulty? The real world still returns in September.

Second, some programs that emphasize self-perception and self-criticism may help, since—as we shall see—inaccurate perception is often a problem. Many programs, however, ignore the fact that some kids with low self-esteem *are seeing themselves accurately.* They feel bad because they know they are not doing well, and children don't have as much choice as adults do about where and how they "perform." Everyday they must manage the academic, social, physical and moral aspects of their lives. Trying to convince them that they are doing better than they are, that they are worthwhile simply because they are human beings, because they are trying, or because no one else is like them, will be rejected as off- target and irrelevant. Kids like results.

Third, therapeutic ideas compete poorly with real-life experiences, especially for children. Ideas may appeal to adults, but self-esteem is a fluctuating feeling boys and girls have while interacting with and trying to manage their world. For children, abstract ideas that border on the philosophical—however worthwhile those ideas might be—are not going to be powerful enough by themselves to have a significant impact on self-concept.

Perhaps the biggest problem with all these efforts to change self-esteem is this: the different approaches may not do much for the kids, but *they do make adults feel better.* It is comforting to think that a troubled child is finally "in a self-esteem program." "I sure hope it helps, because I can't do a thing with him at home!" Unfortunately, however, too often adults don't take the time to carefully think through whether the program is really changing anything. Or worse, they may simply deny the obvious evidence that the youngster and the youngsters's life are still the same. Wishful thinking by adults prevents them from accurately seeing the whole reality of a child's life—and from appreciating it through the child's eyes.

Now that we've described the enigma of self-esteem and examined some of the hopeful but ineffective attempts to deal with it, let's take a closer look at how self-esteem actually operates in the real world. Brace yourself, because coming up next are some facts that you may not want to hear. If you intend to help a child with the revolutionary business of self-esteem, though, you'd better know what you're talking about.

Part II

Understanding Self-Esteem in the Real World

4

Ten Things
You Don't Want to Know
About Self-Esteem

A s we have seen, it's hard for parents and other caretakers to think straight when it comes to the self-esteem of their children. The first requirement for helping children deal with their own self-respect, however, is for adults to understand how the game is really played—not how they think it should be played or how they wish it were played.

For one thing, while you're growing up there are revolutionary changes in the basis of self-esteem every few years. The rules of the game, in other words, keep changing. Children also have to play the game everyday, and they have to play by whatever rules are given to them. There are standards, for example, for school work, for getting along with other kids and for your behavior. You can't change the rules, ignore the rules or make up new ones, no matter how bad you feel.

Taking a hard look at the "laws" of self-esteem can be a little unsettling, though remembering what it was really like when you were a child can help. Walk in your kids' shoes for a mile or so and you will learn—or perhaps remember—the following lessons.

1. Ultimately, the largest parts of self-esteem are earned—or lost—in the big, bad world.

The earliest foundation for self-esteem is the unconditional love and acceptance children receive from their parents. To receive this love, normally, the child doesn't have to do anything other than show up. Good relationships with parents set a precedent for good relationships later with other people. For preschool children self-esteem is usually extremely high. It is not commensurate with their abilities, but this level of self-esteem is fine because it helps youngsters continue to learn and develop.

Once the kids hit school, however, their self-esteem is more under their own control, but it must be earned by succeeding in certain socially valued tasks. The "we love you no matter what" from parents still helps, but now there's more to life than home. The new tasks include academic performance, getting along with others, physical activities and appropriate behavior. Kids have no choice but to accept these challenges. If they are doing poorly, they cannot hide that fact from classmates, teachers, parents or themselves. If they are doing well, on the other hand, the repetition of success with life's critical tasks builds self-esteem and may help "innoculate" a person, to some extent, against future failures.

Earning self-esteem also means that self-respect must be regenerated to a great extent from day to day and year to year. It isn't something you simply have that you can just sit around on. Ask a child who has been sick and inactive for a while—or a mentally alert adult who has just entered a nursing home for the rest of their life—about his or her self-esteem.

2. The Theory of Relativity

"Don't compare yourself to other children; you're only really competing against yourself." This message is only half true. Kids do compare their current abilities to their previous abilities. That is why studies show that, although children's self-esteem drops when they hit grammar school, for most kids it rises, overall, until junior high. Children know they are steadily learning more and more and improving in their own skills, even though they may not be the smartest one in their class.

On the other hand, *it is absolutely impossible for children not to compare themselves to their peers.* By the third grade, children's thinking is well enough developed that they know who in the class is a good athlete, who is a poor athlete, and where they stand in this regard. They know who's a good student, who's not, and how they stack up. Children are always comparing (and so are parents and teachers). Their peers or classmates are a reference group that they use in part to evaluate their own level of success. Telling them not to do this is somewhat like telling them to stop breathing, but it hurts when the comparisons are unfavorable. It also feels good when it goes the other way—when you are doing better than others.

Telling a child not to compare himself to others not only doesn't help anything, it may also make a youngster feel bad about her own character because it communicates that she shouldn't feel competitive in the first place. She is being told that some very strong feelings inside her are out of bounds or wrong. She is also being told not to care about improving herself.

On the other hand, it's quite likely she won't listen much to this kind of advice in the first place. She wants to do well, and—like most adults—judges herself all the time.

3. The Curse of the Uncontrollable

Life certainly isn't particularly fair when it comes to doling out things like looks or brains. Some kids turn out to be cute as a button, and obviously they didn't do anything to earn their good looks. Others are just plain homely. Perhaps most are somewhere in between. Intelligence plays a major role in a child's academic success, and it is strongly affected by heredity. Later in life, studies have shown, both looks and IQ play major roles in career success.

The luck of the draw also affects the kind of temperament a child has. Some researchers have identified three basic kinds of personality that children can have which can be reliably observed from the earliest years. Some kids are restless, excitable and aggressive. Some are shy and tend to be withdrawn. Others have more normal, kind of "in between" temperaments. Each temperament has strong implications for self-esteem. The first type of child, for example, tends to be insensitive and rejected by other children, while the second type tends to be too sensitive and is overlooked.

Self-esteem is also affected by the various events and accidents—good and bad—that life throws at you. These include divorce, the kind of teacher you get in the second grade, the number and nature of the siblings you have, or how often your family moves. It's difficult for adults to admit that sheer luck can have great impact on self-esteem, especially when their own children are involved. It's painful and it isn't fair. Kids, however, live with the reality every day.

4. As you get older, self-esteem becomes harder to change.

This obvious fact is often overlooked, but it has clear implications. Some studies indicate, for example, that self-concept may be pretty well established—barring major upheavals—by the third grade. Accordingly, a child may have fairly clear and consistent expectations of how he is likely to do academically, socially, physically and behaviorally. These expectations can become somewhat autonomous, and, according to some writers, may help to produce "self-fulfilling prophecies." Kids who expect to be rejected often act in ways that produce rejection. Those who expect to do poorly academically may give up more often, resulting in lower grades. Research shows that kids entering adolescence with low self-esteem generally leave adolescence with low self-esteem.

The implications of this are scary. Efforts to establish good self-esteem are critical in the preschool years and in the primary grades. Is it too late after that? Not entirely, but the older a child is, the more dramatic and the more comprehensive efforts will have to be to effect change. Would it be realistic, for example, to expect much from a once-a-week "self-esteem group" for troubled adolescents if nothing else was being done to change their lives? As helpful as the science of psychology can be, we have no way of magically turning on good self-esteem in a seventeen-year-old who doesn't have it already.

5. Parental influence decreases with time.

The basic trust an infant feels toward parents who take good care of their baby is one of the foundations for a good feeling of self-esteem. At this point, as well as during the preschool years, unconditional love and acceptance from parents continues to play a critical role. But once a child hits school, other people—classmates and teachers—enter the picture and have effects on self-esteem that parents cannot control. In adolescence, the influence of close friends and acquaintances becomes extremely important.

As time goes on, therefore, parents' impact on the lives of their children continues to decrease, though it certainly never becomes insignificant. In addition, while the love of parents may in fact be unconditional, the love and acceptance of other people is conditional. You can lose love by doing the wrong thing. Friends can reject you. Husbands and wives can "fall out of love" with each other.

Parents only have so much control over the self-esteem of their children. The kids are not—and never were—just putty in the hands of Mom and Dad.

6. Faulty perception can be a large part of negative self-esteem.

If you are successful, get along well with other people, and behave yourself, you will have good self-esteem, right? Not always. One of the really intriguing questions regarding self-esteem has to do with the fact that lots of people who are, in fact, living their lives well don't have very good self-esteem. They apologize for their successes and cannot understand why other people treat them nicely. They see their achievements as a matter of luck, or worse, they see themselves as somehow putting one over on the rest of the world. And then, ironically, many of these people try all the harder to be successful.

Prejudice is a big social problem. Prejudice is defined as an unfavorable judgment or opinion that is held in disregard of facts that contradict it. *The people we are discussing here are prejudiced against themselves!* They dismiss any successes they experience and they never give themselves a break. Mental health professionals have felt for years that this type of unjustified self-criticism can result from child abuse as well as from the internalization of early, negative parental messages. "I was never good enough to satisfy my Dad. Nothing I ever did seemed to be right." There may also be certain kinds of emotional disorders, such as anxiety or depression, that predispose children to self-prejudice.

Yet whenever misperception is involved in unrealistic self-esteem, it always seems to be unfairly negative rather than unfairly positive. If they're going to mess up their self-concept, people are almost always putting themselves down. They rarely or never—unless they're preschoolers or temporarily psychotic—see themselves as doing much better than they really are.

7. Negative characteristics usually carry more weight than positive ones.

Perhaps this point is related to the last one, because it also has to do with perception. Human beings have always been *problem-solving animals*. We are always much more geared to paying attention to what is going wrong than what is going right. When something's going right, we soon take it for granted. But when something's going wrong, we stew about it endlessly. Out of all the things that happen every day, just look at the ones that editors choose to put on the evening news!

Why is this? From an evolutionary standpoint, it's a very effective way to operate. The theory of evolution, for example, always looked at the adaptive value of any behavior. On this planet any species of animal that was always attending to business and fixing things that were wrong was going to be pretty hard to extinguish. Its members were certainly going to be survivors (think of the ants!). But it might not be much fun to be a member of that species, since you always have to be worrying about something. How about just lounging around for several hours savoring one's most recent, brilliant achievement?

Unfortunately, people don't think like that, and self-esteem, of course, tends to follow suit. People tend to be more taken up with the things that they do wrong, and less impressed with the things they do right. The negative has a natural advantage. When something is going wrong, it tends to take up more mental space and energy, and therefore has more impact.

8. Good self-esteem is not for everyone.

We all want to believe that everyone can or should have good self-esteem. We think a person is somehow entitled to it, and if that person doesn't have it, it should be just around the corner. Maybe we can bestow positive self-regard with a kind word or some liberating insight. Perhaps a weekend workshop will do the job—another Cinderella story at the touch of a psychic button. Perhaps we can produce that wonderful place where all kids are above average.

Unfortunately, this isn't the case. A lot of people don't like themselves and they never will. A lot of them are children, which breaks our hearts but still doesn't make the problem go away. Self-esteem may be a slippery and elusive issue, but it is not magical. In some ways it may even be a spiritual issue, but it still must operate in the real world, and the real world is not fair to everyone. That's why some approaches to self-esteem—religious as well as psychological—try to detach it from what's actually going on in a person's life from day to day. "Don't rate yourself on your behavior," "You're worthwhile simply because you're alive and you're a human being," or "You're wonderful just the way you are."

These ideas are not much of a part of any child's real world. Try to get a youngster to really think that way for more than 30 seconds. For a short while, perhaps, they may actually appreciate the attention involved in a brief pat on the head and a few kind phrases from a well-meaning adult. Then they go back to reality.

9. Some portions of children's self-esteem are based on what people often call "superficial."

It's not uncommon, in reading books about self-esteem, to come across sections describing how kids' self-esteem is partly based on things like physical looks, what kinds of possessions they have, the clothes they wear, where they live or how much money their parents have. Invariably the writer's next comment is that we can excuse these immature and superficial attitudes because we are just talking about young children.

What we have here is a case of "condescending denial." The implication is that by the time they are adults, most people will be basing their self-worth on "deeper," or more significant matters. Not quite. By the time they are adults, people will still be basing their self-esteem—not totally, but in part and at times—on things like money, possessions and looks. Research, for example, has consistently shown that people who are better-looking experience faster advancement in their careers. We also know that poverty itself has a major depressing effect on the self-esteem of those who experience it. Do we need to ask what the $40 million contract does for the self-esteem of the latest NBA rookie?

Though none of this is nice to say, it's true. If we're really honest, we have to admit that there's still a fair amount of the little kid in all of us. We're not going to deal with the problem of self-esteem effectively if we pretend. Self-esteem isn't a religion, it's a down-to-earth phenomenon. You might say it's sometimes deep and sometimes cheap.

10. Snowflakes: uniqueness really means very little.

Kids are sometimes told that there is no one else like them, just as there are never two snowflakes that are exactly alike. There is no one else in the world who looks just like you, talks just like you or acts just like you. This makes you unique, special, neat, wonderful, worthwhile.

It certainly is true that children are unique or special in relation to their own parents. While the fact that everyone is unique may be an interesting concept, however, it really has little relevance to self-esteem. What if you're the best teenage shoplifter in your small community or the ugliest kid on the block? That's unique, but it's not going to contribute to your self-esteem. Uniqueness by itself is a neutral thing. Look at the examples of uniqueness in the self-esteem literature and you'll find that they all involve unique *success* of some kind or another. "Mark was the only child in the fourth grade who could run Lotus 1-2-3 on the computer." Mark is a standout by virtue of his unusual competence compared to most fourth graders. Running Lotus 1-2-3 is not unique at all.

Now that we've taken a look at the "bad news" about self-esteem, let's get a clearer picture of exactly how self-esteem does operate in people's lives. You and your kids wrestle with the problem every day. Let's take an honest look—with no wishful thinking—at how the game is actually played. What we'll find may be hard to swallow at times, but it's fascinating and it may also provide some relief.

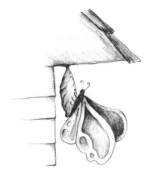

5

The Self-Esteem Revolutions

One helpful way to look at self-esteem—from a not-so-theoretical perspective—is to examine how it develops and progresses over childhood. The topic triggers so much emotion in people that it is hard to just relax and look at it, without letting understandable reactions like compassion, jealousy, distaste for competition or obsession with fairness bias your thinking. Watch your youngsters closely, and you will notice that the basis of their self-esteem will change over the years, and it will also have predictable ups and downs.

There are three primary self-esteem revolutions children experience as they grow up. The first two have to do with the basis or foundation of self-esteem:

1. The first revolution is the change from self-esteem based on *unconditional* parental love and acceptance to self-esteem that is also based on the *conditional* love and acceptance of other people. This subsequent kind of love can be won as well as lost.

2. The second revolution is the change from self-esteem based on *unconditional parental love* to self-esteem that is also based on *competence*. Likf conditional love and acceptance, this kind of self-esteem is earned and it, too, can be won or lost.

The third major change, or revolution, has to do with the development of a force inside the child that really creates self-esteem:

3. The third self-esteem revolution is the transition from a relatively "carefree" existence to the development of an increasingly sophisticated *internal judge*, which we call the Great Evaluator.

In addition to these primary revolutions, there are several secondary revolutions. These are less pervasive, but nonetheless critical. First, fundamental changes occur when the love and competence foundations of self-esteem are further *differentiated* as the child grows older. The love and acceptance dimension, for example, grows to include social skills in early childhood, friendship in middle childhood and romantic appeal in adolescence. The competence domain expands to include self-care skills, athletic ability, academic performance and career choice.

Second, as children get older, revolutions occur in their *ability to think* about themselves. These include their ability to think abstractly about—or "conceive of"—who and what they are, their increased capacity to remember what they have thought in the past, and their strong and innate penchant for evaluating themselves.

Third, from the toddler years on, a major self-esteem dimension is added to the child's life. What starts out as simply the problem of good vs. bad behavior eventually becomes the important quality of *character*, which involves not only moral integrity but also effort, courage and concern for others.

In the Beginning, Ignorance Is Bliss

People aren't born with an innate sense of self-esteem. Positive or negative self-regard, in other words, is not hereditary. Instead, it is something that is both created and learned over the years as a child grows up. It develops from the kinds of experiences kids have, it depends on whether these experiences are good or bad, and it depends on how many good or bad experiences there are.

Right after birth infants don't have a sense of self-esteem because they don't have a sense of self. They arc not aware of being separate from anything or anybody else. They learn they are separate slowly through their five senses, and by banging things around and watching them. Though one important foundation for self-esteem is being laid in the amount of trust they feel in those who care for them and the degree to which they feel loved, to them the world is just one big series of sensations and unconnected events. They smile when they are happy and cry when they are in pain. But they are learning rapidly that there is a world out there for them to interact with.

In the beginning, "self-esteem"—if you can really call it that—is based on parental love and/or the love of other primary caretakers. Then, before the age of two, one of the first self-esteem revolutions gradually occurs: the first manifestations of the dimension of physical mastery or competence emerge. "I am the one who is banging these things around. I can crawl and make noises. I can do things that affect these big people."

As they develop and grow, these little ones are frequently thrilled by their accomplishments. The excitement shown by a twelve-month-old walking across the living room for the first time is a joy to watch. It certainly resembles high self-esteem, but it is a here-and-now affair—gone as soon as you have to change the child's diaper. Whether the toddler-to-be is just excited or really proud of herself, though, is a distinction her delighted parents don't even worry about.

Toddlers have a primitive, simple and very concrete sense of themselves as separate beings. They first learn to describe themselves in terms of obvious, physical things. "I can run," or "I have a truck," is not yet a very elaborate self-concept, but by age two or so, kids know if they are a boy or a girl and have some awareness of their age group. They begin experimenting with separating from their parents or caretakers and operating more autonomously. They can be quite happy and cheerful one minute, and remarkably obstinate and bullheaded the next.

Though not well developed, the self-esteem of preschoolers, in a sense, is very high. In fact, it is unrealistically high. These children are engaging, extremely curious and have boundless energy. They are also very illogical. They are always willing to try new things, and they have an inflated opinion of their skills, no matter what they are doing or how well they have done. They appear almost immune to failure, forgetting it immediately—or not even appreciating it in the first place!—and moving on to the next adventure. This "attitude" serves a healthy purpose, because it keeps them at the job—practicing and practicing the things that they must learn, such as language, physical skills and the ability to tolerate frustration. Their play is their work. Fortunately at this stage most parents are very tolerant of their kids' errors and lack of ability, because they know their children are growing and improving rapidly.

Though high in general, even the self-esteem of preschoolers can have its ups and downs, and after age two another self-esteem revolution takes place. It involves the beginnings of character, as the child begins to learn the difference between good and bad behavior. These young children tend to see things in all-or-nothing terms. Once they understand the meanings of the words "good" and "bad," they may feel one minute they are all good (when someone praises them) and the next minute they are all bad (when someone yells at them). Neither evaluation, however, lasts for long in their mind.

Preschoolers also tend to identify themselves with their physical abilities—what they can do—and they are into independence big-time. They are very proud of their developing ability to care for themselves, and can get angry when parents innocently offer unwanted assistance. Consistent with their visual and physical orientation, they also identify themselves with things like their belongings, family and living quarters.

At this point the child's "self-concept" is not an abstract thought, nor is it remembered from day to day. Self-appraisals are split-second occurrences and then they're gone. This kind of now-you-see-it-now-you-don't self-esteem changes from moment to moment, but it is already based on three things: parental love, physical competence and good behavior.

The sense of competence, however, is primitive. Self-care skills—like tying your shoes and getting dressed—involve real mastery, but many other activities do not. Preschoolers still thrive on arbitrary praise from adults. Feedback just needs to be positive, not necessarily connected to real performance, and it makes little difference what anyone else is doing. For a few brief years, ignorance is bliss.

Fortunately, years of play help give kids the skills that will prepare them for the next huge revolution. For the last time in their lives, the primitive self-esteem of these young children has two characteristics that adults find difficult to understand, or even remember:

1. Self-esteem is not very much related to how well they are actually doing
2. Self-esteem is not much related to how well other children are doing.

School!

About the time children hit first grade, reality strikes its first sizeable blow. The primitive global and uncritical type of self-esteem of the former preschooler takes a beating. Research shows that for most children self-esteem drops significantly when they enter first grade. Because of their amazing adaptability and enthusiasm, however, this setback is not disastrous.

First of all, *self-esteem starts to be related to real performance in the real world*. It is now also based upon competence. Objective standards of the classroom replace wishful, self-congratulatory fantasies. More careful adult observations and feedback replace the pervasive acceptance that was characteristic of most caretakers before. In addition, the jobs or tasks now being evaluated are both required and specific: academic, social, physical and behavioral.

Second, how well a child is doing, in schoolwork or sports or friendships, is measured not just against how well he or she was doing before, *but also against how well other kids in their class or age group are doing*. Life turns out to be a different ball game than was first anticipated! More and more, this kind of relative evaluation is done both by caretakers as well as by the children themselves.

Third, in the interpersonal domain, the unconditional love of parents finds a new mate: *the conditional love and acceptance of other people*, such as peers and teachers. Interactive play, group activities and games are replacing parallel play. Other children can like you or not like you now depending upon how you conduct yourself. Teachers can like you or not depending upon what you're like in their classroom.

For many little first-grade boys and girls this is something of a nasty awakening, sort of like going from Disneyland to Vietnam. The real world does not involve just unconditional love and praise from Mom and Dad. Just trying is no longer good enough. How I actually do seems to make all the difference. And to make life even more exciting, now—in addition to my parents—a teacher and twenty classmates are also watching! Life isn't so simple. It's not just play and it's a revolutionary business.

The First Genuine Self-Concept

Most kids, though, are still up to the challenge and enthusiastically charge ahead. At this time another revolution is occurring in their minds. They are becoming more and more capable of *abstract thinking* and of *remembering* their thoughts. They can begin to understand concepts—what things are and why. They can explain the difference between a tree and an animal. They can also understand the difference between a fir tree and an oak tree, or between a dog and a cat.

Children also begin to apply this new ability to conceptualize to their experiences with human beings. They can tell you the difference between a tree and a human person. They can also begin to appreciate what makes two people different. They know the differences between John and Rebecca, and between Rebecca and Mary.

They also can conceive of and remember the differences between themselves and other children. What "me" means—who and what I am—develops further and becomes more complicated. What I am or who I am has grown beyond just what I can do or what I have. The child becomes more aware that her "me" includes different parts: the social, academic, physical and behavioral (or character) aspects of her existence.

The *social* or interpersonal dimension involves the quality of the child's relationships with parents and siblings. Then it includes relationships with other kids and teachers. How well do I get along with them? Do

I have friends I can play with? What about my teachers—do they like me and see me as cooperative or as a problem?

There is also a major *academic* part to the youngster's life, involving thirty or more hours per week. It's almost like a full-time job. Am I learning my numbers, letters and words? Can I write some of them? How am I doing in relation to the rest of the kids in my class?

Next there is a *physical* realm, which includes appearance, height, weight and build. It also involves athletic ability as well as what some people call "extensions" of the self—clothes, parents, house and other belongings. What do I look like—am I OK or do I think I'm "funny" looking? How fast can I run, and how do I do with the playground games? Do my clothes look nice? Where do I live?

Finally, the child's life has a *character* dimension, encompassing moral integrity and ability to follow the rules. Character might be described as the ability to *do what I don't want to do*, when necessary, as well as the ability *not to do what I do want to do*. Character may also involve how one treats other people, as well as the effort one puts into their activities and, sometimes, the courage required to do things like go to the dentist. Do I get in trouble in class, or do I cooperate with the teacher? How hard am I working? What do my parents think of my behavior at home?

In the primary grades kids are starting to conceptualize and remember these different parts of themselves. Social, academic and behavioral dimensions of life are emerging in addition to the older predominantly visual and physical aspects. With these abstractions about themselves, children are now forming and remembering their first real self-concepts. This is me; this is what I am.

Here Comes the Judge

For each child, the period of time around third grade—about age eight— is momentous, because, fortunately or unfortunately, as soon as self-concept is out of the gate, it is closely followed by an internal judge. This is the third primary self-esteem revolution. The *Great Evaluator* has appeared—the creator of self-esteem—who from now on will accompany the child almost everywhere. Life doesn't allow you to merely have a complex self-concept, *it also requires that you appraise it.*

Self-appraisal is not imposed on children by adults, as many people think. It is true that adults also do their share of evaluating kids, but a large part of the evaluation comes from within the child. It's as if the child wakes up one day and finds a new guest in his head.

Introduction from the Great Evaluator:

I figure I should introduce myself to you, since I'm going to be with you for the rest of your life. I'll sort of be your coach while you're growing up. You're probably not really surprised, because I think you've noticed me hanging around more and more recently.

Growing up is a pretty hard business. I'm going to be here to help you along and kind of give you some encouragement. I'll be with you—kind of in the back of your mind—wherever you go. I'll be there in your work, and sometimes—for a while—in your play. And I'll guarantee you I'm not one bit lazy! I'll work hard for you—and on you.

I have to warn you that you won't always like me. When you're trying real hard and doing well, I'll see to it that you feel real proud of yourself. You'll love it! But when you're not doing so hot, I'm going to make you feel bad. You won't like that at all.

I'm not doing this to hurt you. (Remember we have a job to do here —it's called "growing up"—and I'm stuck with you, too.) When you've done well and I make you feel good, it's so you'll want to do well again and again. When I make you feel bad, I'm doing it so you'll remember to try harder the next time and avoid the mistakes that got you in trouble. That's what a coach does. You'll get the idea. I have a lot of confidence in what both of us can do working together. I'll do my part and you'll do yours.

You already know that other people are very important to you. I'm going to help you with them, too. Part of my job is to help you remember what other important people tell you about yourself. That's another way for you to learn and to do better.

Don't worry, I won't be driving you crazy all the time. There will be times when I'll leave you alone. You'll probably enjoy most of these times, but I won't take that personally. I'll rest or something.

But I'll always be back to give you a push, because what you've gotten yourself into here is no cakewalk. It's not so easy. Sure, it can be a lot of fun, but most of the time you have to earn what you get. No one's going to hand you a great life just because you tried, or just because you showed up, or just because you're a human and didn't happen to come out a turtle. Big people like to tell you "nice" things like that sometimes when you're upset, but they're not true. It's tougher than that. You won't have good friends, do well in school, stay out of trouble and learn to be on your own simply because you're a person.

By the way, this is my first job.

Well, that's enough chatter. I think we both know the rules. Let's get on with it.

The Coach. The Motivator. The Magistrate. He lives inside. The blissful innocence of the preschool years is gone forever.

The arrival of the internal judge, however, is not really bad. Kids have a ferocious desire to grow up, and they instinctively insist on keeping track of how they're doing. That's natural enough, and the judge is part of that process. You'll never get better at throwing darts if you're blindfolded and can't see where your shots go. So this internal judge serves a constructive educational and motivational purpose. He tells you where you are and compares it to where you want to be.

We'll describe the purpose and nature of the Great Evaluator more thoroughly in the next chapter, but for now let's just say his job is to make kids acutely sensitive to how they're doing in the social, academic, physical and character arenas. On these aspects of their lives they compare themselves to others all the time, and school provides perhaps their chief proving ground.

Junior High Crash

The increase in social, academic, physical and character "self-esteems" continues for the majority of children until they hit junior high (sixth or seventh grade). Then, in what is a kind of repeat of the transition to first grade, reality dishes out another shock. School transitions are always hard for kids, but this one may be the worst because it involves a number of unsettling changes—both internal and external. Self-esteem again drops significantly, especially, as we shall see, for girls.

In junior high each boy and girl now has seven or eight teachers, as opposed to one primary teacher and a few others for music, art and gym. The school itself doesn't just seem huge, it *is* huge. There are tons of other kids, perhaps 800 to 1,000 compared to the old school that had only 300. The school is also physically large, and students must also move from class to class—quite quickly, as a matter of fact—during the day. The emotional support of the one teacher who knew you well is replaced by a new feeling of anonymity. Counselors are available, but they're buried in the maze somewhere and you have to go find them.

In addition, academic self-esteem gets shaken because academic standards are tougher and there is more work. You also have to be organized. Boy, do you have to be organized! You have to know which books you need for which class, how to take notes and where to keep them, and how to keep track of what homework is due. Teachers seem less forgiving of mistakes and more demanding. To many kids it feels like they are working harder than ever, but no one seems to care or notice.

Social self-esteem also takes a beating. The school is enormous and the bedlam at passing time sounds like World War III. Buried in this new mass of humanity are former friends from the earlier grades, but it feels like everyone is a stranger. Most are. New junior high students understandably feel like they don't know anybody. Making matters worse is the fact that beginning junior high students are around age twelve—incipient adolescence—so they are starting to feel more shy and self-conscious. The new school accentuates these feelings. It also means that a new, exciting, but very stressful self-esteem dimension is entering the picture: *romantic appeal.* Who likes whom? Who's cute and nice and who isn't? Who's dating? Who's going to like *me*?

Life will never be the same.

In 1987 the research of Roberta Simmons and Dale Blyth, described in their book, *Moving into Adolescence*, pointed out that self-esteem takes more of a beating when a number of important developmental changes occur *at the same time*. In addition to the changes mentioned above, these kids are also at the time of life when they are undergoing the internal biological and physical changes associated with puberty. What am I do to with this new body of mine and with these new feelings?

Since girls start this process, on the average, two years earlier than boys (around age 11 for girls, 13 for boys), they are more often the ones who have to deal with it while also trying to manage all the other changes. This, according to Simmons and Blyth, is why their self-esteem takes much more of a dive upon entering junior high than does that of the boys. The interesting and sad part of this, these authors point out, is that many of these girls don't really recover from the setback. For many self-esteem remains at a lower level in the following years.

Bumpy Road in Adolescence

With regard to self-esteem, adolescence itself is a time of excitement, intrigue and threat. With senior high, another major school transition and, for some, the continuing physical changes that signal the revolution from childhood to adulthood bring with them another challenge to self-esteem. Self-concept—and indeed one's whole life—goes through a terrific physical, psychological and emotional reorganization. Although many researchers now seem to agree that the teenage years are not usually as stormy and traumatic as they have often been portrayed, they are a time of erratic moods and self-esteem highs and lows.

As it is for younger children, self-concept in adolescence also continues to be affected by academic performance and physical abilities. The competence revolution continues. Issues having to do with character also become increasingly important, as adolescents are often demanding idealists. But perhaps the main reason self-esteem becomes unsteady is social. Adolescents feel more social sensitivity and self-consciousness than they will ever feel at any other time of their life. The interpersonal revolution, from dependence on parents to attachment to peers, is in full swing.

Teens feel the whole world is watching everything they do. As they mature sexually, they no longer have just neutral feelings toward the opposite sex, and the self-esteem equation is thrown out of kilter by the new factor of romantic appeal. Physical attractiveness becomes more important—especially for girls—and teens can be extraordinarily touchy about minor physical traits that they may perceive as undesirable. Self-esteem can be crumpled by the thought that your nose is crooked, your ears are too big or your breasts are too small. The Great Evaluator can be quite fickle at times.

The social sensitivity of teenagers also has a lot to do with the emphasis they now put on friendships. The influence of family dimin-ishes, and having friends, getting along with them and keeping them becomes an extremely important component of self-concept and self-esteem.

Teens' self-concept becomes further differentiated because now they are also capable of thinking of themselves and others as having a certain kind of "personality." I am not just what I can do or what I have or what I look like, but I am also a person who has a certain way of operating in the world and a certain way of getting along—or not getting along—with others. I now also evaluate myself in terms of my ability to be fun, kind, loyal, cool, smart and interesting.

Another new self-esteem component is the teen's growing aware-ness that he will not be living with his parents all his life. He'd better start thinking about work and career, a major factor in what is often described as defining one's identity. Career selection and career plans—like roman-tic appeal—become a significant new dimension in the self-esteem picture.

Interestingly, the self-esteem of adolescents shares three character-istics with the self-concept of preschoolers. For one thing, it tends to be based on a feeling that is very egocentric—the whole world revolves around me. For the preschooler this results in a positive, energetic attitude. For the teen, however, it means alternating excitement and self-conscious-ness. Second, both preschoolers and teenagers have self-concepts that are somewhat out of touch with reality. The preschooler, fortunately, seems immune to failure. Teens are not immune to failure, but they are idealists and dreamers. They have new-found mental abilities that allow them not only to think abstractly, but also to imagine different possibilities for many things. These things include not only the ideal world but their visions of their own futures. For many teens their self-esteem is partly determined by the possibilities they see for themselves later in their lives.

Finally, like preschoolers, adolescents tend to see themselves in all-or-nothing terms, especially in the interpersonal arena. I can be cool one minute and a jerk the next. The highs and lows produced by the Great Evaluator are especially extreme. Teens see themselves as walking perilously close to the edge of a cliff. One minor slip-up and you can fall into the Valley of Eternal Dorkdom.

Does self-esteem, then, generally go up, down, or sideways during adolescence? Some studies seem to indicate that, in spite of everything, after the drop in early adolescence, self-esteem improves. Parents may sometimes forget what is was like, but for their teens there is a tremendous amount to be accomplished during the adolescent years—all to be done against a backdrop of constant change and insecurity. If self-esteem does, in fact, improve for most kids over this period of time, it is once again testimony to the incredible flexibility, enthusiasm, and perseverance of children. They have a great tolerance for revolutions.

One of our main characters, the Great Evaluator, made his momentous appearance in this chapter. His job is a critical one as far as self-esteem is concerned, and it deserves further clarification.

Summary:
Self-Esteem Revolutions in Children

The Three Primary Revolutions:

Basis of Self-Esteem:	Later Expands to Include:
1. Unconditional parental love	Conditional acceptance of others
2. Unconditional parental love	Competence
3. No inner judge	Internal judge capable of conceptual thought and memory

The Secondary Revolutions:

The *Social* dimension expands to include:
> Same-sex friends
> Romantic appeal ("personality" plus body image)

The *Competence* dimension expands to include:
> Self-care skills
> Academic performance
> Work and career

The *Physical* dimension expands to include:
> Athletic skills
> Self "extensions," e.g., family, belongings
> Body image

The *Character* dimension expands to include:
> Moral integrity
> Effort
> Courage
> Concern for others

6

The Great Evaluator

S ome people don't care much for the Great Evaluator. Some don't even want to admit he exists in each and every child. Why do little children have to be judging themselves all the time? Why can't they just play and enjoy themselves while they're still young, and not be loaded with emotional burdens and responsibilities? Isn't the Great Evaluator really the beginning of the perfectionism and destructive self-criticism that so many adults inflict on themselves?

These worries are both understandable and legitimate. The first recognizes our wish to see our children enjoy their childhoods. On the other hand, it misses the fact that in their play and in their lives in general, kids have a primary job, and that is to grow up. The Great Evaluator is there to help that task along.

The second concern, though, recognizes the fact that the internal judge inside children isn't the most reasonable creature in the world. He's a bit like a loose cannon in the beginning, and *under certain circumstances—which we'll describe later—the Great Evaluator can definitely go haywire*. As a motivator he is not initially objective or reasonable, and he can become a critical tyrant or can be rendered basically inoperative by certain unfortunate events. But the Evaluator is there, and each judge in each child needs help from objective and sympathetic adults, like parents and teachers, to do his job right.

The Great Evaluator—this internal appraisal mechanism in the young child—is the creator of self-esteem. Too often we take the phenomenon of self-esteem for granted. It's just there; what else is new? Self-esteem is self-esteem and, of course, it's great if it's good, even better if it's high, and rotten if it's low.

If you really think about it, however, why should self-esteem exist in the first place? What good is it? Do animals have self-esteem? Why can't people just go along, live their lives, take care of business and enjoy themselves without *worrying all the time about how well they are doing?*

The Great Evaluator creates self-esteem in children for two fundamental and basically constructive reasons: *efficient learning and strong motivation*. He's there to facilitate growing up. He creates self-esteem—that is, the good or bad feelings that follow an action—to add efficiency and force to the drive to master the difficult developmental tasks that face children—tasks like getting along with others, academic learning, mastering the environment, developing character and becoming independent. He makes kids care—and care a lot. Self-esteem to growing up is like fertilizer to a plant or a half-time pep talk from a coach to his team. It is a catalyst—extra insurance to see that the job is done, and done well.

Efficient Learning

The Great Evaluator provides blunt and consistent feedback to children about how they are doing. No holds barred. There is always a detailed focus on "How did you do?," "What did you do well?," "Where did you fail?" It seems most everything is reviewed. The evaluation flows automatically.

Kids do this to themselves. They are amazingly intense and energetic. They are always curious about how they are doing, and they definitely want to improve and to do things right. So the Great Evaluator makes children sensitive to how they perform in school, how well they get along with peers, how appropriate their behavior is and how hard they try. Focusing on feedback makes learning more efficient because it allows individuals to try something, see how far off target their performance was, make adjustments and then try again. You never improve at anything if you're always shooting in the dark.

Strong Motivation

In addition to the goal of efficient learning, the Evaluator also helps "jump start" the young child by providing some real emotional force to the struggle of growing up. He creates powerful motivation by stimulating in children extremely strong—and very often exaggerated—feelings about their success and failure. For most kids, though, he is a friend to their fierce and unwavering desire to grow up and master their world.

How exactly does the Great Evaluator motivate? He borrows from a biological and evolutionary principle of survival. Have you ever noticed that one good thing about the design of human beings is that activities that are important to survival are naturally enjoyable? The human organism has evolved in a way that helps insure that necessary functions will be taken care of. That's why eating when you're hungry and sleeping when you're tired feel good. It's probably also why sex and—sometimes even exercise!—feel good. It's a clever idea: *If it must be done, make it pleasant.* Nature also makes not doing what you're supposed to do feel bad—like starving or trying to stay awake at midnight when you're exhausted.

When a child is doing something well and experiencing success, the judge inside produces a wonderful feeling—that is the feeling of high self-esteem. The excitement at young ages is exaggerated—precisely for motivational purposes. Watch little kids and you'll see it. "Wow! I did it! Mom, watch this!" For a short while the youngster is ecstatic. What they did may not really be a big deal, *but to them it is.* Later, of course, the child is strongly motivated to get more of that wonderful feeling— the "natural high" of self-esteem—by continuing to struggle, learn and master the social, academic, physical and character tasks that are such an important part of their life. The Evaluator uses this conditioning process to see to it that there is zest and excitement in what is a difficult struggle.

That's what self-esteem is for: to make sure a difficult job—growing up—gets done. If self-esteem didn't exist, many of the tasks would probably be avoided. Growth would be slowed or perhaps even stopped.

But the Great Evaluator also motivates in another way, which is why some people get nervous. When a child is doing poorly, the judge inside creates a painful feeling—the feeling of low self-esteem. This feeling is frequently exaggerated in the young, but this is also done for motivational purposes. The "Wow! I did it! Mom, watch this!" may be replaced by "Wow! What a jerk I am. I hope nobody saw that idiotic blunder!" Embarrassment, silence and withdrawal may follow for a while.

This is not tragedy, however, for the embarrassment is usually short-lived. *The Great Evaluator also intends that failure motivate*: "I don't ever want to feel like that again, and I'll work my tail off from now on to avoid it!" This is constructive motivation and it is a natural part of life. That is why "feel good learning" approaches that attempt to protect kids from all failure are missing the point entirely.

The Evaluator's Defect

The Great Evaluator, therefore, is both a facilitator of learning and an ardent motivator. Together with reasonable and caring adults he can do a lot of good. But he has one big flaw. He is not especially bright. It's like it's his first job. He is not scientific or objective, and he is sensitive to influence from other people. He takes feedback, passes it on to the child and remembers it. He does the best he can, but critical thinking is not one of his strong points.

In doing his job the Evaluator often tries to incite, arouse, inspire and encourage by overstatement. He can use extreme, overgeneralized, all-or-nothing language. He makes a child feel "absolutely super" when she accomplishes something. She feels her success was "totally awesome," when in fact it may not have been that stupendous. But that's OK; she'll work to get more of that ecstatic feeling.

The Great Evaluator can also make a child feel miserable when she fails. His embellishment of simple mistakes may seem to topple her into the gloomy valley of instant incompetence, idiocy and social ostracism. This is not being fair or objective either, but it's done to stimulate the effort which, when blended with learning, will help prevent similar failures in the future. There is no getting around the fact, however, that these moments of failure are very painful to children, and the danger here is that *if the Evaluator's exaggerations are frequently reinforced by important adults in the child's world, permanent self-prejudice can occur.*

Though the Great Evaluator's main function is to insure the child's future success and happiness, he can be strongly influenced by other people. For one thing, the self-esteem feeling he creates—whether positive or negative—is always enhanced by the presence of an "audience." For another thing, The Evaluator is dumb in the way a computer is dumb. The principle is "garbage in, garbage out." He is especially prone to pass along to the child—and to remember well—certain kinds of feedback. He is very impressed by three things:

1. Important people
2. Repetition
3. Strong emotion

Here is where there is potential for trouble. The Evaluator can be impressed, unfortunately, *whether or not the feedback is correct or accurate.* In this respect, both he and the growing child are naive and immature.

Evaluations and comments from parents, teachers and other significant others in the child's life flow into the child's awareness every day. Sometimes they can temper the Great Evaluator's tendency to exaggerate, in which case the child may learn the beginnings of compassion or real humility. On the other hand, information from adults can sometimes reinforce the Evaluator's distortions. When this happens in a negative direction, over time the Great Evaluator may become the Faultfinding Tyrant.

The Great Evaluator, and the self-esteem he produces, are a catalyst—a function of the young child's mind that serves to promote learning and enhance motivation. The internal judge can be groomed and nurtured to everyone's benefit, or further distorted to the detriment of the child.

7

The Nuts and Bolts
of Self-Esteem: I

Though the notion of self-esteem may sometimes appear sublime, it's really a very ordinary, imperfect and down-to-earth business. Self-esteem itself is a changing feeling—good, bad or somewhere in between. It comes when the Great Evauator in a child (or in an adult) judges that person's worth, goodness or competence in relation to some dimension of life. If the evaluation is positive, the person feels good for a while. If the evaluation is negative, she feels bad. For most individuals, there will also be many times during a typical day when they are not evaluating themselves and, consequently, when a sense of self-esteem does not exist.

These evaluations are ideas, and if you add them all up, they are sometimes referred to as one's "self-concept" or "self-image." But keep in mind that they vary somewhat depending upon the situation, area or task being evaluated. A self-concept is a bunch of conclusions or judgments I make about myself. It might involve ideas such as "I am likeable," "I am quite overweight" or "I am persistent." The feeling of self-esteem results from the kind of conclusion I make at a particular time. If my conclusions generally are positive, you might say I have good self-esteem. If they are mostly negative, you could say my overall self-esteem is poor.

What Is Being Evaluated

A natural part of being a human being is to feel good or worthwhile—or the opposite—based on your evaluation of yourself with regard to life's essential dimensions or tasks. This kind of judgment is inevitable and spontaneous. In addition, as we have seen before, after about age eight the evaluation is more complex and abstract. It is also remembered more and more and it is based on what we are actually doing in the real world.

What are the important tasks or essential jobs life presents to us? As mentioned, the following areas are extremely important to human beings—and to their self-respect: (1) *interpersonal relationships* with family, teachers, friends and others, (2) *competence*—the ability to solve problems and to master things like school or work, (3) *physical realities* like appearance, health, athletic abilities, body image, and belongings, and (4) *character*—moral integrity, courage, effort and concern for other people.

Children who evaluate themselves positively with regard to interpersonal relationships might entertain the following self-concepts:

> My parents think I'm a good kid.
> I'm good at making friends.
> Other children think I am fun.
> I'm nice to kids I don't know that well.
> My teacher likes me.

These thoughts or concepts, when activated, would produce good feelings. A child's "social self-esteem" would be positive.

Children with poor interpersonal esteem, on the other hand, might think the following things about themselves:

> My parents yell at me a lot.
> I don't like to meet new kids.
> Other kids tease me every day.
> I wish I had more friends.
> My teachers think they have to keep an eye on me.

When these thoughts are operating in the child's mind, they would generate uncomfortable or sad feelings, which would be the essence of poor social self-esteem.

For children, self-esteem in the competence domain involves primarily academic performance. Kids with good self-esteem here might think:

I like school.
My report card is usually one of the best in the class.
My parents are proud of my schoolwork.
I feel good about my math and spelling.
I like to read a lot.

Kids who are struggling academically might think the following:

I don't like to go to school.
My teacher doesn't think I'm a good student.
I hate math.
I don't care how I do in school.
My parents always nag me about my homework.

Self-concept in the physical arena can involve physical talents and appearance, as well as some "physical extensions" of the self that include belongings as well as identification with other family members. Good self-esteem here might involve the following thoughts:

Other kids think I'm nice-looking.
I'm good at most sports.
My new computer is really cool.
My parents like to watch me play soccer.
My mom has a real important job.

Poor self-esteem on this dimension, on the other hand, might go something like this:

Other kids think my clothes are ugly.
I feel stupid when I try any sport.
I'm too chubby.
Kids tease me for the way I look.
My dad doesn't have a job.

Finally, there is self-esteem related to character. Here we run into two problems. On the one hand, kids who follow the rules and show considerable effort don't often think about it. They usually take for granted the fact that they stay out of trouble or work hard. On the other hand, children who have trouble in this area often blame it on others and may actually maintain, in some ways, an unrealistically positive self-concept. Whether realistic or not, however, positive self-concepts related to character might include:

I don't give my parents or teachers a hard time.
I work hard on my schoolwork.
In volleyball I try as hard as I can.
I can do things even if they scare me.
I do what I think is right.

Negative self-concepts related to character might include:

I'm always getting in trouble at school.
I'm lazy.
When it comes to sports, I don't care a lot.
My parents usually think I'm a problem.
I often feel ashamed of myself.

Looking at these four areas, it is apparent that self-esteem and self-concept have a definable scope. They also have different "parts," depending on what he is doing or thinking about at the time. At any one time a person may be judging himself on interpersonal self-esteem or perhaps on competence esteem. At other times both dimensions might be involved in the same activity, such as a cooperative learning group in the classroom which involves both the social and academic realms.

To make things more complicated, each of these "parts" probably has different parts, too. The social domain includes relationships with a spouse, siblings and parents, acquaintances and close friends. The competence dimension includes work, school or hobbies. The character area includes effort, guts, moral values and kindness.

As kids get older, the different dimensions can also overlap. In the grammar school years the competence and physical areas are combined in athletic ability. In the teen years the social and physical dimensions will help produce the quality of romantic appeal. In those same years the social, character and competence areas help to produce the feature often referred to as "personality."

Notice the difference here between these real-life dimensions and some of the abstract self-esteem "solutions" that are sometimes proposed to children. "You're a wonder just the way you are," "I'm terrific," "I LIKE ME!," "My value is unconditional and can't go away," or "I'm unique—there's only one person like me." These statements may have some validity as abstract ideas, but they come across as out of touch with reality of kids' lives. For young children self-esteem operates at a concrete level first, then it slowly evolves to include more conceptual thought. Yet self-respect never loses its connection with its original, down-to-earth roots. Right at this moment, 10:35 AM on Tuesday, April 10, I can't do my long division problem, and I know that everyone else is already done.

At different times, therefore, the Great Evaluator may be doing his evaluating on different aspects of a person's self-esteem picture. Therefore, the feeling of self-esteem will usually be changing to some extent. If we say someone has good self-esteem, though, we often mean he rates himself high or adequate in most or all areas. The reverse would be true for low self-esteem. And, of course, there are also people who have high self-esteem in one area and low self-esteem in another. You might call these different patterns "self-esteem lifestyles."

Self-Esteem Lifestyles

Self-esteem is a dynamic, shifting entity. For any one person it will vary during the course of a day, week, month or year, but may still have some predictability or consistency. If we look at individuals from the point of view of how they are doing in each of the four self-esteem dimensions, we readily find that there is a tremendous amount of variability across different people. Some people experience consistent satisfaction, some persistent distress and some unsettling change.

For some people self-esteem will vary minimally through all four dimensions, but it will remain at a consistently high average. Mary, for example, is ten. She sees herself as fun to be with and as an easy person to like. She also enjoys reading and likes school as well as her teacher. She is well coordinated and is a star player on her soccer team. She works hard at most things she attempts and stays out of trouble. Her self-esteem profile (a bit oversimplified) would look something like this:

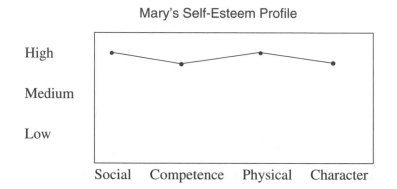

Mary's Self-Esteem Profile

For other people, self-esteem will vary minimally through the social, competence, physical and character dimensions, but it will remain consistently low. At age thirteen, Mike is an anxious young teen, but wishes he had more friends. School is difficult for him, and he often feels teachers don't like him. He is poorly coordinated and is aware that he looks very awkward when he runs. He avoids taking risks at all costs and prefers TV to homework. His self-esteem chart might look like this:

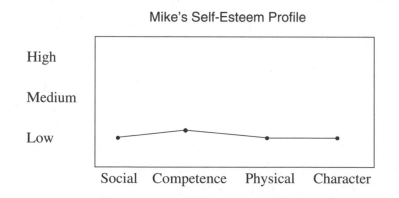

Mike's Self-Esteem Profile

Finally, there are people for whom self-esteem is generally consistent within a dimension, but quite inconsistent across dimensions. Sarah is an aloof and distant child with no real friends. She is intellectually gifted, however, gets straight As and consistent positive feedback from her teachers. She is overweight and does not like sports at all, but never gets out of line and works extremely hard on her schoolwork. Her profile would look like this:

Sarah's Self-Esteem Profile

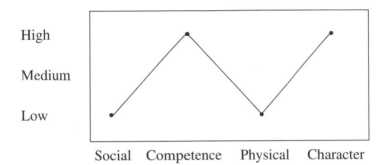

What does Sarah think of herself? It depends on the moment you ask her. Unfortunately, however, most people have a tendency to dwell more on their faults while they take for granted their good points, so—with her social and physical weaknesses—her overall self-esteem might still tend toward the negative.

You might have noticed that something was left out of these examples. In each we assumed that the Evaluator was objective—that the reality and the child's perception were the same. This isn't always the case. Carl, for example, in reality has characteristics very similar to Mary's. He gets along well with his family and has a number of friends. He is an excellent student, a standout performer at several sports, and very conscientious and hard working at whatever he does.

If we look at Carl's self-esteem chart, however, we have to make a distinction between how Carl is actually doing (REALITY) and how he thinks or feels about himself (PERCEPTION). Let's imagine that the solid line represents the reality of his accomplishments and qualities, and the dotted line represents Carl's self-perception:

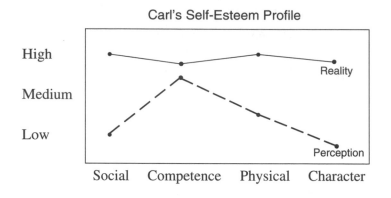

Carl's Self-Esteem Profile

Carl's Evaluator is not objective. Carl, for some reason, often feels lonely and sometimes takes innocent comments from other people personally. He is rather perfectionistic and sees himself as an average to slightly better than average student. He is acutely aware of—and remembers for a long time—any mistakes he makes during a basketball or baseball game, and never gives himself credit for being a hard worker.

Carl's self-esteem is out of line with reality. His Great Evaluator has gotten off course somewhere. This will be one of the problems we'll look at later .

"Global" Self-Esteem

What about "global" self-esteem? Is there such a thing? Is it possible for a person to add up all the different aspects of himself and come up with some kind of total picture or summary?

Perhaps the best answer is that global self-esteem is a score on a self-esteem questionnaire. Some of the items from Coopersmith's questionnaire, for example, sound like they might describe a kind of summary judgment about oneself. On the positive side, we have statements such as:

I'm pretty sure of myself.
I'm pretty happy.
I can usually take care of myself.
Things usually don't bother me.

On the negative side, on the other hand, we have items such as:

I'm a failure.
I often wish I were someone else.
Things are all mixed up in my life.
I have a low opinion of myself.

Adolescents and adults are more capable of spontaneously doing this kind of self-evaluation. Younger children respond to items like this if they are asked or are presented with them, but they are less likely to think them on their own.

How does a person come up with a global impression of himself? Self-esteem is bit like arithmetic. If he is asked, for example, what he thinks of himself, an individual might "add up" or "average" all his self-judgments to come up with a global impression. He might "scan" the various dimensions of his life. He might also attribute different weights—or importance—to different dimensions.

In the cases of Mary (all positive) or Mike (all negative) described above, adding up or averaging is easy to do. What happens with global self-esteem, however, in someone like Sarah, where there is a combination of positive and negative factors? We really don't know for sure, but there is a good possibility, for the reasons we mentioned earlier, that the negative factors—the "unfinished business"—might dominate the global impressions. This would be especially true if Sarah, for example, in her own mind really felt that the social domain (one of her weaknesses) was more important than the area of competence (one of her strengths).

In their daily existence, people may at times have a kind of background sense of overall self-esteem, but normally they will very likely be feeling the specific results of one or two dimensions at a time. When their competence esteem is active, for example, their physical esteem may be dormant. When their character esteem is activated and they are feeling guilty because they did something wrong, their interpersonal self-respect may temporarily be forgotten.

Who Is Doing the Judging

Throughout one's life, there are two basic sources of feedback that help create self-esteem. One comes from other people and the other comes from inside a person himself—from his own Great Evaluator. When kids are toddlers and preschoolers, they are inexperienced and learning, so an important feedback source is—as Cooley and Mead said—other persons: parents, teachers, friends, relatives. As they grow older, though, their Great Evaluator appears, and they generally become more capable of having their own opinions about things, including opinions about themselves. The result is that their self-esteem becomes an integration of both sources.

Some people, for various reasons, wind up more sensitive to the opinions of others, especially in certain situations. Other people are able to weight their own opinions more heavily. But just about everybody takes both sources of information into account.

It is important to keep in mind, however, that for everybody, ultimately, the final judge is inside themselves. The main reason for this is the simple fact that they are not with the other people all the time, but they are with themselves constantly. At these times any judgments from other people are reduced simply to memories that can be forgotten or recalled depending upon the orientation of the judge within. It is the Evaluator inside—like it or not— that must ultimately make sense out of a person and his world.

8

The Nuts and Bolts of Self-Esteem: II

We're beginning to see that the nuts and bolts of self-esteem are an ordinary, though changing and complex, business, but there are still other questions to be answered. If self-esteem depends upon self-evaluation, how is the judging done? Does competition play any legitimate role? What determines the intensity of self-esteem at any one moment? Can there ever be times when self-esteem isn't present? And what's the final verdict on the cause-and-effect question?

How Is the Judging Done?

If you're going to judge your performance on something, how do you know how well you're doing? You must have some criteria or standards. Basically, there are two ways to tell:

1. Internal reactions (satisfaction or frustration)
2. Comparisons with:
    (a) your own previous performance
    (b) the performance of a "reference" group
    (c) the performance of another person

Internal satisfaction. In the social area immediate internal reactions often determine self-esteem to a great extent. It feels good, for example, simply to have a friend. During a moment of closeness or shared fun with someone important to you, you naturally feel good about yourself. It's like the Great Evaluator is saying, "This experience is good, and you're good, too." You may feel even better if a month previously you didn't have any friends (comparison to your own previous performance), but it may not make any difference at that moment whether you have more friends than someone else (comparison to others). Who cares about the rest of the world right now? The spontaneous, internal satisfaction is what counts.

An internal reaction of satisfaction might also create a good feeling of self-esteem in an adult who is just getting back to work after a two-month illness. No comparisons to what anyone else is doing are necessary or particularly relevant at the moment. It just feels good to be able to go back to work.

Comparisons to yourself. People also make judgments—and thus determine a level of self-esteem at certain moment—by comparing themselves to a standard based on how well they've done in the past. If their Evaluator feels they're progressing at a fine clip, they feel good. If you're forty-two years old, for example, and after four months of weight training you can now do twice as many reps as you could in the beginning, you may feel ecstatic and your self-esteem may skyrocket. Your physical esteem is dominant at this moment. This feeling may also be enhanced by internal reactions (the endorphins are flowing!), but at that moment it doesn't make much difference to you that professional athletes can press hundreds of pounds.

Comparisons to a reference group. You can also compare yourself to a group standard: what you think is good or poor performance for a group of people that are similar to you. A reference group may be similar in things like age, sex, job, or they may be members of the same organization, social class or team.

Imagine, for example, that you're a good athlete in general. You're also twice as good a football player as you were last year. You're still on the varsity B Team, though, and even though you're on the B team, you're not playing much. In this situation your physical self-esteem may be low because you are comparing yourself to the varsity squad where you want to be. You may, in addition, be seriously considering quitting the team. Even though you're doing a lot better than you were earlier (competition with yourself), what is having more impact on you is the unfavorable comparison to *your* primary reference group (the varsity football team).

This example also demonstrates another interesting aspect of self-esteem: its "upwardly mobile" character. For self-comparisons, people tend to choose reference groups that are performing better than they are. People also tend to ignore reference groups that they see as inferior to themselves (e.g., the B team or all non-football players in the school), even though these groups may—for comparison purposes—have a logical connection to the individual who is doing the comparing. This "upwardly mobile" aspect of self-esteem makes the job of feeling good about oneself harder, but it's easy to see in it the motivational working of the Great Evaluator: push, push, push.

Comparisons to other individuals. Finally, you can also compare yourself to another person. This type of comparison can be helpful, but it can also be dangerous. If the person you compare yourself to is a kind of model or even hero for you, your emulation of that person may spur effort, achievement and personal growth. If, on the other hand, the other person is a sibling or a peer, the comparison may simply feel like envy and aggravation, and it may provoke unrealistic discouragement rather than motivation.

William James, whom we mentioned earlier, comes to mind in this regard. You may remember he said, quite candidly, that his self-esteem depended upon his chosen profession (psychology), or what he "backed [himself] to be." That's fair enough. He went on to say, however, that if he perceived that another psychologist was doing better than he, he would be devastated. This extreme kind of reaction doesn't always happen, but it can, and it clearly underlines the danger to self-esteem that is often involved in comparing yourself to *one* other person. You may wind up putting yourself down unfairly, and lose the perspective that results from comparing yourself to a reference group or to your own previous performance.

It is interesting that because James made this statement, however, many subsequent writers have used his words to try to separate self-esteem from competition entirely.

The two kinds of comparisons (to self and to to others) often operate together in the same situation. For example, when young children hit the primary grades, as mentioned earlier, their self-esteem takes a bit of a dive, because they are suddenly being compared on their academic, social, physical and behavioral functioning to their classmates. They weren't used to having a reference group. But up to the junior high years (grades 6-8), their self-esteem in general rises. This, obviously, can't be due to their all being at the top of their class. Instead, part of their self-esteem is *also* due to the fact that their Great Evaluator is comparing them to *their own* previous performance. They themselves are getting better and better.

Some of the dimensions mentioned before are heavily affected by this "competitive" quality, and some aren't. The competence and physical dimensions are evaluated a lot on the basis of comparison to one's prior self or to reference groups. Fourth graders, for example, are sensitive to how they compare academically, while adolescents are closely examining things like looks, body image and personality.

On the other hand, the social and character dimensions are not as often evaluated in these ways. In the interpersonal domain, sometimes kids will count friends and compare the numbers, but more often they are focused on the friendships themselves. And as far as character goes, most children follow the rules fairly well, so that factor often drops out as a meaningful basis for comparison.

The important thing to keep in mind is that *part of self-esteem depends upon competition*—competition with your former self and competition with other people.

The Intensity of Self-Esteem

Self-esteem operates by its own intriguing laws. The intensity of the self-esteem feeling, for example, can depend on several things:

1. The value of the task or area to the person
2. The perceived degree of success or failure
3. The nature and size of any audience present

Value. The more important a valued area is to a person, the stronger she feels—good or bad—about how she is doing. If I don't value athletics very much, whether I'm on the football team will not affect my self-esteem a lot. But if I have gone to all the trouble to get on the team and I fumble the ball during a game, my self-esteem will take a dive.

As we mentioned before, kids don't have a lot of choice about the tasks in life that they value. Among other things, for example, they have to go to school. Many teachers today worry, however, that children don't value education and academic effort the way they used to. They are saying, in other words, that it's not as connected to self-esteem as it used to be.

Perceived degree of success. How large or small an individual perceives her success or failure to be also impacts self-esteem. The area may be important, but if the victory is seen as relatively small, the impact on self-esteem won't be great.

The way people perceive things can sometimes be very strange. Different Evaluators in different people can have relaxed, rigorous or even harsh standards. Some individuals, who tend toward the perfectionistic, can't tell the difference between a small failure and a large failure. They simply feel like an idiot when there is *any* failure. These people often discount the good things they do, minimizing effort and maximizing luck.

Audience. Another interesting factor that frequently affects self-esteem is the size and nature of the audience that is witness to a person's success or failure. The bigger the audience, the stronger the feelings. Even if the event is not a big deal, it may feel like one if a lot of people—especially important ones—are "watching." If you hit a home run at your little league game, it's a big deal. It's a bigger deal if your Mom, Dad, older sister and best friend are watching.

Of course, there are also plenty of times when there is no audience factor at all. In the depths of the night you finally factor that last stupid algebra equation. You've stuck it out for three hours and finished all your homework. It's just you and your Great Evaluator. As a matter of fact, a part of character we'd all like to see more connected to self-esteem is the ability to show guts, effort and moral integrity *when no one is watching*.

It seems these days that sometimes the fact of having an audience has almost become a valued dimension in itself. This is a little scary. Look at the apparently large number of people who are willing to reveal all kinds of terrible things about themselves, whose primary motivation is simply to be on TV or, in other words, to have a large audience. It sometimes appears that our society is becoming more audience-driven than driven by things like achievement, kindness or character.

No Self-Esteem!

Can there be times when self-esteem isn't activated—when it doesn't exist, either in a positive or negative way? The answer is yes. The Great Evaluator does take some time off. There is no law that every human being on earth is required to be evaluating himself twenty-four hours a day. In fact, the times when you don't evaluate yourself can be some of the most pleasant moments of your life.

Moments like this occur, for example, when your attention is totally taken up with something fascinating or enjoyable. After her homework is done, one little third-grader is watching her favorite movie. She is not evaluating herself at all. A starving teen takes the first bite out of a thick mushroom and sausage pizza. He's evaluating the pizza instead of evaluating himself. Another adolescent is hanging on for dear life on a roller coaster. A middle-aged gardener, on a mild spring morning, notices for the first time that his tiny green cabbage sprouts have popped through the ground.

Here the event—not the me—is primary. "How am I doing?" has no meaning, and a person just enjoys life itself. Reference groups, previous performances or the achievements of other people have no meaning for a while. Moments like these capture the essence of "play" in its most positive sense. It is important to remember that self-esteem is only one of life's satisfactions.

Durability

It certainly appears that self-esteem, once established, tends to be durable and consistent. Research has indicated, for example, that those who enter adolescence with low self-esteem leave adolescence with low self-esteem. Some writers have interpreted this as due to what is often called a "self-fulfilling prophecy," i.e., people tend to behave in ways that are consistent with their self-image.

Yet, it is apparent that even "problem" children still want to do well in school and get along well with other kids, even if they have had a lot of negative experiences previously. This is, in fact, a large part of what makes low academic or social self-esteem so painful to kids—they are not achieving what they want.

Another explanation may account for the durability of self-esteem. This explanation is compatible with the idea that self-esteem is more a result than a cause. *Self-esteem tends to stay the same because the things that produce it stay the same.* Things like social skills, academic performance, physical looks and ability, and character do not often change very much or very quickly. Kids who see themselves as having no friends, getting poor grades and being the last one picked for playground games have low self-esteem for good reason. *They are seeing themselves accurately.* Their skills and resources are often lacking. They very much *want* to do better, but realistically they have no rational basis for expecting or hoping that they *will* do better.

On the other hand, those who are successful in these areas will continue to maintain high self-regard because *they have every reason to believe that their skills and resources will not suddenly abandon them.* This often seems highly unfair, heartbreaking and offensive, but it is the way things are. The "haves" continue to have and the "have nots" continue to have not. Changing poor self-esteem, when it exists, will be a major undertaking.

In short, self-esteem is a catalyst and a kind of barometer. As a catalyst, it adds spark to the young child's growing up, but it can only work with the resources the child has as far as social skills, competence, physical attributes and character are concerned. It does not have a lot of power in and of itself.

As a barometer self-esteem is a kind of imperfect indicator of how things are going in someone's life. It is more of a reflection of life than a force in itself. Self-esteem is still important, though, because it can be a kind of warning light to point out where there might be problems that need to be dealt with.

And just as a real barometer can produce inaccurate readings when it is damaged or defective, the sense of self-esteem can be faulty when the Great Evaluator inside a child is biased.

The Bottom Line on Self-Esteem

Let's now look at the question raised before: what's causing what? Is self-esteem a by-product of the quality of one's life, or is good or poor self-esteem, in itself, the cause of a satisfying or unsatisfying existence?

We have looked at self-esteem from the point of view of a child's daily life in the real world. In doing so we have tried to eliminate denial, wishful thinking and the tendency to try to use abstract ideas as emotional painkillers.

We have thus seen that positive *self-esteem is primarily the result of two things: real world success and a fair internal Evaluator*. "Success" is a multifaceted affair and for most children, fortunately, the range of acceptable performance is fairly broad. Success—or lack of it—occurs in the dimensions of interpersonal relationships, competence, physical attributes and character. Self-esteem, therefore, will sometimes be based on things that are under an individual's control, but at other times it will be based on things that involve only luck. Sometimes it will be based on things that people consider admirable and almost noble, such as effort and self-sacrifice, while at other times it will involve things that people consider superficial, such as looks and physical possessions.

Because self-esteem is multifaceted, in any one person it changes some from time to time, in some people varying tremendously, while in others remaining consistently high, medium or low across the various dimensions. Self-esteem may most often depend upon what children are doing at the moment, but as they get older they develop more and more of an ability to "sum themselves up" in their minds.

This attempt to sum up one's whole self is often referred to as "global self-esteem." Given the fact that self-esteem is complex and changing, how can a person draw a conclusion about her entire self? When someone is asked what she thinks of herself, or when she hears her name, she may attempt to "scan" the different dimensions of her life, "add" them up, and come up with some kind of conclusion. Scanning, however, is very prone to bias. In some people, for example, self-concept and self-esteem can be unrealistically low because the scanning process repeatedly gets "stuck" on a particular negative dimension.

This is one form of self-prejudice, which we'll discuss more in the next chapter, and it underlines the fact that good self-esteem depends not only on doing well, it also depends on one's Evaluator being able to appreciate this success.

9

Self-Doubt—
Right or Wrong

After taking a down-to-earth look at the mechanics of self-esteem, we have a clearer picture of what is required for a child to have adequate self-respect: reasonable success and an objective internal judge. Reasonable success means adequate performance—not necessarily stupendous—with regard to the social, academic, physical and character aspects of one's life. Unfortunately, kids—unlike adults—must deal with all of these dimensions simultaneously. Unless the Great Evaluator is intolerant, though, the range of tolerable success levels is a fairly broad one.

It's amazing, given the magnitude of the tasks facing them, that children are so enthusiastic about attacking and continuing with the job. Watch a class of little first graders coming to school in the morning. You are first impressed with their energy and enthusiasm on the playground. We older folks can get tired just watching them! Then observe as the bell rings and they abruptly switch gears and head for the classroom, where they demonstrate their willingness to sit still, follow instructions and tackle their schoolwork. As we have already seen, though, as children get older their self-concepts become more complex and—in spite of their enthusiasm—their self-esteem has predictable ups and downs.

There are also other things that can go wrong for individual children—things that compromise success and/or lower self-esteem in one area or another. Before saying someone has a "problem with self-esteem" and trying to do something about it, it is very important to "diagnose" what kind of self-esteem problem it is. There are three basic things can that can generate significant self-doubt in an individual:

1. Accurate perceptions of weakness
2. Inaccurate perceptions of weakness (self-prejudice)
3. Negative global esteem (self-condemnation).

Self-esteem enhancers sometimes forget that children's self-esteem will always be lowered when the child *accurately perceives* that she really does have a problem. This was the case with Sarah in the last chapter. On the other hand, self-prejudice can occur when a child *exaggerates* a weakness or sees one that isn't there, as Carl did. And finally, self-esteem can be almost nonexistent when—for various reasons—*pervasive self-condemnation* is present. Here the Great Evaluator has become "unhooked" from the individual's successes and positive attributes. Unable to appreciate them, he is incapable of generating good feelings when good things happen.

Accurate Perceptions of Weakness

The first kind of self-esteem problem is the *accurate* perception by a child of a *real* weakness. He sees something that impairs his performance, success or satisfaction with one or more of the self-esteem dimensions—interpersonal, competence (academic), physical, or character. He may observe that he is frequently criticized by his parents, extremely slow when it comes to reading, the last one chosen for team sports activities, or easily frightened and unwilling to attempt anything that he feels is new and risky.

The important point with this first type of problem is that the Great Evaluator is pointing out to the child a weakness that really exists. Sarah, from our previous chapter, had a self-esteem profile that looked like this:

Sarah's Self-Esteem Profile

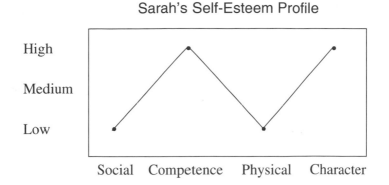

Social   Competence   Physical   Character

Other children see Sarah as detached and rather cold. As a result she has no friends, though at times she would like to. She is extremely intelligent, however, and gets straight As. At other times she uses her intelligence to criticize—in her own mind—other children of whom she is jealous. Sarah is between chubby and fat, and she tries to avoid athletic activities at all costs. As far as her behavior goes, though, she never gets out of line and works extremely hard on her schoolwork.

Sarah is intelligent and sensitive. Her recognition of real areas of weakness results in her feeling the pain and discomfort of lowered self-regard every day. She has a self-esteem problem because she has real problems to be concerned about. Imagine trying to boost Sarah's self-esteem by telling her that she's unique, or that she shouldn't compare herself to other kids, or that she's "a wonder just the way she is." Sarah knows what the deal is. She can feel on top of the world when the math and spelling tests are handed back. After that, though, comes gym.

Problems with any of the four dimensions can lower self-esteem to some extent. This may simply be demoralizing to a child. If the child sees the problem in question is modifiable, however, the Evaluator may try to use the discomfort to provide motivation to change. This would be a test of the youngster's character.

Interpersonal Difficulties

From a social perspective, research has often found it helpful to think of children in terms of three catergories: accepted (well-liked), overlooked (withdrawn) and rejected (aggressive). Studies suggest that a little less than half of all children fall in the first category, generally getting along with others. They have their uncharacteristic moments, but overall they learn how to give and take in ways that allow them to have satisfying and fairly lasting relationships. In this domain they may not need a lot of help or coaching from their parents. Their social self-esteem is adequate to good.

As Karen Owens points out in an excellent book, *Raising Your Child's Inner Self-Esteem*, research has shed some light on the characteristics of children who are well-liked. They tend to be extroverted, honest, cheerful, and cooperative. They can be aware of and responsive to others' feelings, which makes others see them as thoughtful, giving and capable of sharing. Interestingly, well-liked children are also usually respected for strengths in two other self-esteem domains: academic and physical. Kids who are good athletes and good students also tend to rate high in popularity and peer acceptance.

Children who fall in the overlooked category are often shy and withdrawn. Perhaps fifteen to twenty percent of our youngsters fall into this group. They tend to be anxious, insecure and sometimes depressed. They do not enter readily into conversations or group interactions, and their moods can be changeable and often negative. The result is that they wind up being unpopular, though it may be more accurate to say they fade into the background and are socially isolated.

The social self-esteem of overlooked/withdrawn children, therefore, is generally low and remains that way unless something dramatic happens to involve them more with other people on a regular basis. These kids are often aware of—and very frustrated with—their social limitations.

Ten to fifteen percent of children fall into the aggressive or rejected category. These kids are bossy, impatient, and intrusive. They tend to develop bad reputations that are hard to shake and their social skills are poor. They are not sensitive to others' feelings, are often uncooperative and frequently imagine hostility in the actions of others when it isn't there. Aggressive/rejected children usually do poorly in school and are often defiant with adults. They have the poorest prognosis of any of the three groups.

What about the social self-esteem of the rejected/aggressive child?

Adults have for years assumed that it had to be negative. How could any child feel good about himself in this area when he treated others so poorly and had so many negative experiences?

Well, the Great Evaluator, as we pointed out before, isn't perfect. This may be one of the rare times where distorted, unrealistic perceptions produce positive self-esteem. Recent research seems to indicate that if you ask these children how they get along with others—or what they expect going into some social situation—they respond positively. They see themselves as having friends and relating well to others!

This response is very puzzling. Perhaps these kids are not telling us the truth. Or perhaps, since they are unable to reflect on their experience, their social self-esteem becomes dominated by wishful thinking. Unfortunately, whatever they think when they are young, their problems often catch up to them as they get older.

You may have noticed that the percentages mentioned for the three groups above don't add up to one hundred percent. This is because not all kids fall neatly into one of the three groups, since they have qualities of two or more of the categories described.

As kids get older, they become more and more aware of, and involved in, the social scene, and peers become more and more influential in their lives. This trend culminates in adolescence, where teens are exquisitely sensitive to this social dimension. Adolescents value friendships and romantic appeal very highly, and if their Evaluator sees problems in those areas, the effect on their self-esteem can be devastating.

Academic Problems

For adults the biggest test of their competence has to do with their primary job or career. For younger children their biggest test is academic performance in school. Early in the primary grades, kids find out that positive feedback is no longer arbitrary. Their achievement in reading, writing and arithmetic is now tied to objective standards monitored by people called "teachers," and it is also related to how well other children are doing. It all adds up to significantly more pressure.

As we have seen, most kids do well enough that their academic self-esteem continues to improve after the initial shock of entering the primary grades. Adults often forget, though, that for kids school is a full-time job, and when academic problems occur, they put stress on a huge portion of a child's life. Many therapists have seen youngsters who are really struggling academically and who have a kind of *school-related depression.* Their moods are noticeably better on weekends, vacations and summertime, and noticeably darker when school is in session. In these situations, academic self-esteem is usually poor and going to school feels like a daily assault.

Studies have also suggested that by third grade—around age eight—academic self-esteem may be becoming fairly well established. In other words, kids by this time have developed fairly durable thoughts about whether or not they expect to succeed or to do poorly in school. It is not accurate, though, to think of academic self-esteem as the chief determinant of a child's success in school. Many studies have shown that the relationship between self-esteem and academic success is rather weak.

Instead, it might be more realistic to think, first of all, that ability and effort expended on schoolwork produce academic performance, like this:

Ability + Effort > Academic Performance

Academic performance, in turn, especially early on in a child's school career, helps determine academic self-esteem. The situation would look like this:

Academic Performance > Academic Esteem

An interesting cultural difference appears with regard to this formula. Asian children, teachers and parents tend to believe in the power of *effort.* They think all children can do the work if they try hard enough. Though this is not true, everyone (parents, teachers and kids) believes it. This conviction is part of the reason that, overall, Asian students do so much better academically than American students.

What do Americans believe? They tend to think that academic performance is more due to one's *fixed intellectual ability* level. They underestimate the importance of effort. Research has shown this belief tends to produce less effort and more discouragement, especially in the face of frustration. If I'm not doing well and it's due to a fixed trait that I can't change, why try harder?

The reality is that academic self-esteem in the early years is mainly the product of academic performance. There's nothing to go on before that. Unconditional parental love may be important, but it's in a different realm than academic performance. This is what the second primary self-esteem revolution is all about. In the early grades the Great Evaluator examines the child's actual achievement and gives the feedback that generates good or bad self-esteem feelings. Academic performance itself, however, is a result of both ability and effort. Apparently Americans underestimate the contribution of effort and Asians underestimate the contribution of ability.

Anything, therefore, that lowers ability or impairs effort will be likely to cause trouble and stress. The list of culprits here includes learning disabilities, below-average intelligence, Attention Deficit Disorder and emotional problems such as anxiety or depression. Kids, of course, don't know what these problems are. But they do know when they're not doing as well as their classmates.

Physical Issues

This is one of the self-esteem dimensions that adults have a good deal of trouble understanding from a child's point of view. Parents and teachers forget that little kids are very visual, physical beings, and that their physical self-esteem depends on several things:

1. Looks, or physical appearance
2. Coordination and athletic skills
3. Self "extensions," such as belongings and family

Adults have trouble admitting that these factors are tied to self-esteem for a couple of reasons. First of all, looks, coordination and self-esteem extensions are largely matters of sheer luck, and as such are not readily modifiable by either children or parents. You can only do so much to improve how cute or attractive you are. Though body weight can be modified some—especially earlier in life—facial features and body build are largely givens. You can also practice and practice at a particular sport, but for many kids their innate level of fine and gross motor coordination limits the activities that are available to them. Quite understandably, when their children's self-esteem is concerned, adults can't stand being confronted with the Curse of the Uncontrollable.

Another reason adults can't appreciate what physical self-esteem in children is about is that they quickly tend to label it as "superficial." It is probably true that most of us are not as good-looking as we'd like to be, so what better strategy than the "sour grapes" routine? It really doesn't matter that much in the first place—other things in life are more important. *For self-esteem, they say, let's make a new rule: we'll only count the things that we can control.*

So adults try to see children's preoccupation with looks, athletic skills and belongings as trivial. They attempt to unhook self-esteem from these physical characteristics, making vague pronouncements like, "It's what's inside you that counts." The result? The adults feel much better in their self-constructed fantasy world. The children, however, remain in the real world, where how good-looking they are, how fast they can run and what kind of house they live in mean something.

Questions of Character

One definition of character is the ability to either (1) do something you don't feel like doing or (2) not do something you do feel like doing. Either is done—or not done—in the service of a value or long term goal. Character, therefore, involves both effort and self-control. Effort can be mental, as in doing two hours of boring homework or confronting something that scares you, like giving a speech. It can also be physical, like running a cross-country practice on a hot day when you're feeling exhausted and no one's around to cheer you on. Self-control might involve avoiding sex at an inappropriate time, not screaming at someone who's just insulted you, or avoiding a delicious piece of banana cream pie while trying to lose fifteen pounds.

Factors that can cause problems in character development include innate temperament, poor discipline and parental modeling. Some children who are born with very difficult temperaments also seem to have trouble with effort, perseverance and conscience development. Not all these youngsters, of course, will continue to have character flaws as adults, but their negative tendencies can be exacerbated by inconsistent or overly permissive discipline. These tendencies are made even worse if Mom or Dad also model poor character traits themselves.

Do people with these difficult temperaments have lower self-esteem? Oddly enough, as we mentioned before, they may not. People with severe character problems often fall into the rejected/aggressive category, and they are notoriously unreflective. Their Great Evaluator is either drowsy or asleep most of the time. As a result, they may have some awareness of their problems, but The Evaluator may not trigger a lot of guilt, concern or desire to change.

On the other hand, as we have also mentioned, it seems that those who exercise good self-control and put forth lots of effort often take these virtues for granted. They may admire these positive traits in someone else, but they ignore them in themselves. When they do something wrong, however, their self-esteem can be devastated. *The tie between character and self-esteem, in other words, is there, but the link appears to be weak, erratic and illogical.*

One of the antagonists to character self-esteem, therefore, is the tendency of people not to appreciate themselves when they are expending considerable effort or self-control. How unfortunate! It would be helpful if we could come up with some ways for parents and teachers to help children give themselves a pat on the back when they are doing well in this regard.

To a large extent, many of the writings on self-esteem have attempted to address this issue. The messages of McKay and Fanning in *Self-Esteem*, of Bednar and Petersen in *Self-Esteem: Paradoxes and Innovations in Clinical Theory and Practice*, of Ellis and Harper in *New Guide to Rational Living*, and of Brandon in *The Power of Self-Esteem* are similar. If you're going to evaluate yourself, they say, judge yourself on the one thing you can control: your character. What is most important is your integrity, effort and courage—not outcomes or results.

This message is motivational and inspiring, and these days especially it is more and more needed, though more and more neglected. Character is—or should be—a critical part of the self-esteem equation. Unfortunately, these writers leave behind is a bit of reality. People always have, and always will, evaluate themselves on *results* as well as effort. Both character and actual performance—or outcome—are part of the self-esteem picture.

In an excellent book, *Greater Expectations*, which focuses a good deal on character development in children, psychologist and educator Bill Damon of Brown University recognizes this fact. We must "present children," he says, "with high standards and expectations that can inspire them throughout their lifelong development." Typical self-esteem programs, he feels, offer nothing but a "mirage" that children find meaningless, because in the real world they are focusing intently on "...what they look like, what they do, where they come from." We would do better, he points out, "to help children acquire the skills, values and virtues on which a positive sense of self is properly built."

Inaccurate Perceptions: Self-Prejudice

Another fairly common problem with self-esteem occurs when a child holds inaccurate perceptions of himself. He sees weaknesses that don't exist or exaggerates ones that do. The Evaluator, in other words, has somehow gotten fouled up. A "self-esteem problem" here results from something that the child thinks or perceives diminishes or devalues him in one or more of the four self-esteem dimensions, when in fact this isn't really the case.

This was the problem with Carl:

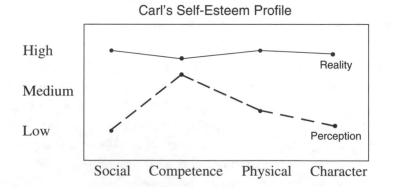

Carl's Self-Esteem Profile

Carl, as we saw before, got along well with family and friends. He was an excellent student, a star performer in several sports, and very conscientious and hard working. If he were able to appreciate the reality of how he was doing, his self-esteem would look like the top (solid) line in the chart. Carl's Evaluator, however, is not objective, and his perception of himself is represented by the lower (dotted) line on the chart. He sometimes feels lonely and takes things too personally. He demands perfection of himself, and consequently feels that anything less than straight As isn't good enough. When it comes to sports, he remembers well any mistakes he either made or almost made, and he usually sees himself as not working hard enough.

Carl is a classic example of self-prejudice. In spite of the evidence, he generally thinks more poorly of himself than he should. Other examples of self-prejudice? A cute sixteen year old girl who feels unattractive because she keeps thinking her nose "looks like a ski jump." She maintains this perception in spite of the fact that innumerable males of the species pay plenty of attention to her. The excellent student who once again dreads a geometry test—in spite of his 97% average in the course and the fact that he studied six hours for the exam. A sensitive eleven-year-old girl who often takes the lack of a smile on her teacher's face as a sign that she's done something wrong.

The important point with this second cause of self-doubt is that the Great Evaluator—for some reason—is pointing out to the child a weakness that does not really exist. As it is with the first kind of problem, this misperception also results in the pain of lowered self-esteem. And just as it is with real problems, this erroneous thinking may be discouraging, or it may provide motivation to change, even though there is nothing that needs changing.

We probably don't understand all the causes of self-prejudice. It very likely occurs when the judgments of the Evaluator become skewed due to either innate temperament or due to the influences of other people. As the creator of self-esteem, the Great Evaluator is a function of the child's developing mind. As such, it is also developing with the child, but its operation can become biased or even extremely distorted.

The Evaluator is full of energy and the desire to motivate and teach, but he is a bit like a rabid high school coach with an IQ of twenty. He motivates in part by exaggeration. Thus, the younger they are, the more kids tend to think of themselves in extreme terms. They get more excited about their successes and more shattered by their failures. If the child's natural temperament is very intense or anxious in the first place, or if significant people in the child's life also give feedback in extreme or distorted terms, trouble can follow.

Remember that the Great Evaluator is impressed by three things: important people, repetition and strong emotion. He has a tendency to accept as valid, in other words, feedback that comes from people like parents, teachers and peers. Accurate or not, this feedback will be more likely to "sink in" the more it is repeated and the more it is accompanied by strong feelings on the part of the person giving it.

Self-prejudice can develop, in other words, if kids often hear from important adults messages such as:

"What's the matter with you?!"
"I see some Bs, but don't see any As."
"When are you going to learn?!"
"Let me do that for you."
"I'm sick and tired of you whining all the time!"
"You got a brain in there or not?"
"That was really dumb."
"Get over here and listen to me, young lady. I've told you a million times..."
"This isn't a very good job—where was your head?"
"You're never going to amount to anything."
"I'll do it myself. You always mess things up."

Self-prejudice can also develop in the absence of positive feedback. Unlike those in the examples above, some parents and teachers are not overly harsh, but they tend to give only feedback that is corrective. Praise is foreign. Their philosophy is that you don't expect a pat on the back for just doing what you're expected to. All an Evaluator hears, therefore, is criticism, which he is inclined to remember and pass along.

Self-prejudice is certainly a problem, because it causes unnecessary internal pain. However it often involves an ironic twist. Folklore—or folkscience—has always claimed that low self-esteem produces frustration and poor performance. Certainly, as Bandura pointed out, this can be true when someone with low self-regard gives up easily. But the irony here is that self-prejudice can also be one of the strongest motivators known to man, sometimes stimulating a never-ending struggle to prove oneself and, as a result, amazing accomplishments. Perhaps we don't know as much about self-esteem as we think we do.

Global Self Condemnation

For most children, as we have seen, self-esteem tends to be unrealistically high till about the time they enter school for the first time. Then they realize that there are other kids out there and that they will be "graded" for their actual performance—not just for showing up or trying. In spite of these new challenges, most children continue to progress and self-esteem rises until the next big school switch.

Some kids, however, never get a chance to enter the self-esteem competition on a par with their peers. The initial self-esteem revolutions involve the transition from unconditional parental love to conditional love and competence. The victims of physical, sexual or emotional child abuse never receive unconditional love in the first place. Early on life throws them a nasty curve that they may not be able to understand at all on any intellectual level. They can "understand" their mistreatment very well, though, on an emotional level, and what they "understand" or feel inside is that *they themselves are bad*. Their Evaluator has become "unhooked" from their actual success, performance or effort. No matter how hard they try, they don't feel entitled to feel good about themselves.

Much as we don't like to admit it, for many youngsters this devastation to self-esteem is permanent, except perhaps for those who are able to have access to—and benefit from—group and/or individual psychotherapy.The effects of early abuse—sexual, physical or emotional—can be crippling for the following reasons:

> 1. From an early age kids have some awareness of
>   good vs. bad behavior, but at that stage they can't

separate themselves from their observable behavior.

2. When there is a problem, children assume that adults are right and they are wrong.

3. When abuse occurs early, the child's first impression of herself is that she is very wrong (or bad) or always wrong (or bad).

4. Most kinds of child mistreatment are not one-time incidents, they are repeated occurrences.

5. Most kinds of child mistreatment also involve important people and strong emotions.

This kind of negative, global self-esteem can continue to contaminate a person's perception of herself for years to come. No matter how well she is actually doing, she may feel that she doesn't deserve her success, that she is really some kind of fake, and that she is not worthy of others' attention or love. For many of these people, self-esteem is about as close to zero as it can get.

As Susan Forward said in *Toxic Parents*, the results of abuse are remarkably similar for different individuals. "They almost all feel worthless, unlovable, and inadequate," she says, and as adults "the resulting lack of confidence and self-worth can in turn color every aspect of their lives."

Part III

Managing
the Self-Esteem
Revolutions

10

Parenting Basics

If self-esteem depends on success and a fair Evaluator, the job of parenting is clearer. Parents need to help promote social skills, competence, physical development and character in their children, and they must help the kids judge themselves fairly and accurately. How is this to be accomplished?

Mom and Dad must first have a *philosophy* of parenting that will encourage the development of a positive self-concept in their child. They need to have an idea of what they are doing. Next, they need to understand the impact their *relationship* with the child has on the child's growing self-respect, interpersonal skills and underlying sense of worth. Here the notions of liking and modeling are critical.

Parents must then *understand* the massive changes, or revolutions, that self-esteem goes through as their child matures. They also need to appreciate the nuts-and-bolts of self-esteem as it operates in the child's world, not in a world of wishful thinking.

Finally, parents must have the *self-control* to be able to manage their own feelings, especially anger and anxiety. These emotions, when mishandled, pose a serious threat to the objectivity of the Great Evaluator.

A Parent's Mission Statement

As we mentioned earlier, a reasonable philosophy of parenting provides for both the self-discipline and the self-esteem of children. It borrows from the helpful work of Coopersmith and Baumrind, and it acknowledges that kids are going to grow up in the real world. It might read something like this:

My children didn't ask me to, but I chose to bring them into the world. What I've gotten them into is an adventure and a joy as well as a struggle. My job is to prepare them for it—and to enjoy them while they're here with me. Eventually, though, their lives will require that they live together with other people, eventually work in some way, take care of the only body they'll ever have and maintain considerable self-control.

I will do my best, therefore, to offer them the following things. I'll commit myself to giving them what they need to get started and I will be committed to their successfully leaving me someday. I will always be committed to their welfare, but I will not accept everything they do. My job is to provide them the basics—food, shelter, clothing and warmth, but it is also to teach them how to live. I'll teach them rules and values, and expect them to abide by them. I will also give them freedom to explore their own interests and ideas within the limits that life and society provide.

I will try to become expert in being a parent. I can't instruct my children well unless I have confidence in myself as their guide. My job as a parent will not be simple, either from an intellectual standpoint or from an emotional one. It will be complex and will often produce significant emotional strain on me. This I'll try to see as a normal part of the job. At certain times I will be required to provide firm discipline and, at other times, warmth and affection.

I can't do everything for my kids. I couldn't even if I wanted to. Most of their work and suffering I can't take away from them. At times, in fact, I will have to be the one who triggers their frustration and tears. I realize that their self-esteem will come partly from how I accept and treat them now, but later—when I am less important to them—it must also come from their being able to live their lives well.

I want my children to be successful and to be able to judge themselves fairly. I know they will be their own judge soon enough, and I want the judge inside them to be fair and reasonable. I want their judge to push them, but also to be compassionate when they make mistakes. They don't have to be the best in everything they do, but they still must do well.

There's a lot of work to do in any walk of life, but I also want my kids to have times when they don't judge themselves at all, good or bad. I want them to be able to play—as children and later as adults—and to have times when they simply enjoy being alive. I want them to experience the fact that, although it's important, there's more to life than self-esteem.

I will continue to be aware that my children will leave my unconditional acceptance and love for a world where love is conditional and competence is required for self-respect. My job is to help prepare them for these basic revolutions in their life.

The Parent/Child Relationship

The first primary influence on a child's self-esteem is his relationship with his parents. The child/parent connection forms the basis for future relationships, in a sense telling the child what can be expected from other human beings and also teaching him how to behave in a good relationship. In the very beginning a child's security and sense of worth will be very much affected by how much he feels accepted and cared for (loved) by his parents and how much he feels liked. (That's why good discipline is important: you won't like a child who's driving you crazy all the time.) Later, another important parental influence will enter the picture: parental modeling.

There has been a good deal of disagreement about the concept of unconditional acceptance, or unconditional positive regard from parents. Some have argued that a child needs to be accepted no matter what he does, but this view really makes no sense. Part of a parent's job—as we'll see when we discuss discipline—is to teach a child that rules and limits exist and will be enforced consistently. What kids really need for their self-esteem, therefore, is not an unconditional license to do whatever they want. What is more appropriate, as Diana Baumrind points out, is a parent's unconditional, enduring *commitment* to their welfare. The child's early sense of worth will depend a lot on the perception that his continued well-being is one of his parent's most important objectives. This is one definition of love.

Yet love is not the whole story. A child's self-esteemwill also be affected by how much she simply feels *liked* by her parents. People often forget how important it is to feel liked, in addition to being loved. A parent who enjoys his daughter, and who spends time with the child because of this, communicates many things: "You are worthwhile," "You are fun," "You are likeable and loveable," "I want to be with you," "You make me happy," and "I'm glad you came along." These statements are very powerful self-esteem builders. It is very difficult, on the other hand, to foster the self-esteem of a child whom you don't like.

Many parents love their children, but don't like them. They become so focused on their efforts to care for their kids and to promote good behavior that they overlook the fact that the relationship has turned sour. This misdirected focus hurts everyone's self-esteem. Hassles over getting up and out in the morning, sibling rivalry or homework can produce consistent and intense frustration that blocks all positive feelings. Lectures, nagging and arguments can come to dominate the parent/child interactions. On the other hand, parents who can establish discipline routines that are friendly but firm, consistent and supportive will have a better chance of fostering the performance they want from their children, while at the same time continuing to like them.

Another fascinating result of studies about self-esteem reveals that parental *modeling* has a strong influence. This conclusion is not so surprising, really, because we have long known that children imitate their parents in many ways. Kids also tend to imitate the self-esteem levels of their parents. In other words, young boys and girls see their parents showing the characteristics of high-self-esteem persons: decisiveness, kindness, effort, positive relationships with others, staying in shape, being active in things outside the home and confidence in their own abilities. Sons and daughters then tend to take on these characteristics themselves.

Understanding Self-Esteem

It is also important for parents to understand how self-esteem actually operates in children. That way they can be more sympathetic to their kids as well as more realistic in their expectations. On a hot Saturday afternoon in July twelve-year-old Tom comes marching in the door and slams his baseball glove on the floor.

> Mom: What's the matter?
>
> Tom: We just lost the stupid game! Those idiots scored four runs in the last inning. Our pitcher is a complete dork!
>
> Mom: Now, that's no way to talk. Curtis is a nice boy. Here, have some orange soda; you look beat!
>
> Tom: No thanks.
>
> Mom: Well, don't blame me for your game! I wasn't there. Besides, the most important thing is that you guys played hard, not whether you won or lost.
>
> Tom: Gee, that's great—a whole new perspective! Wow! Now I'm actually glad those guys won!
>
> Mom: You know that's not what I...
>
> Tom: (interrupts) Yes, yes—now I've got it! They can be happy they won, and we can be happy for just showing up! Something for everybody. Gee, that's really stupid!

An unnecessary clash between a gentle, well-meaning parent and an aroused Great Evaluator. What's the lesson here? The Great Evaluator is a Great Exaggerator! What's needed is an understanding of the self-esteem battle from the boy's perspective. He doesn't really believe his friend is a jerk. Mom might have been better off saying, "That's a shame," and then saying nothing. Things will soon calm down. Self-esteem fluctuates, as we have seen, and *when it is low, people tend to be irritable and often want to be left alone.* Tom's self-esteem here is temporarily at low ebb and he's sore. For motivational purposes his Great Evaluator is torturing him some, but it won't last long.

What good does your understanding self-esteem do for your child and for you? For one thing, when the kids are frustrated, it allows you to appreciate what they are going through and not say dumb things to them that will only cause further aggravation. It also allows you to relax more when confronted by an overly frustrated child, because you can see the motivational workings of their inner magistrate. Very likely the agony you see now will motivate the child to try harder in the future, in part so they simply won't have to feel that way again.

Understanding self-esteem can also allow you to have realistic expectations for your children's behavior, and to understand at times why he is doing what he is doing.

> Dad: Knock off the Nintendo and get in here for
>   dinner! That's the fourth time I've had to tell you!
> Jeff: OK, OK, OK. (Keeps on playing.)
> Dad: I SAID NOW, YOUNG FELLA! Do I have to
>   come in there and drag you to the table?!
> Jeff: (Sulks in to dinner.)

For Jeff playing Nintendo is one of his higher self-esteem activities. He's skillfully obliterating the evil sector of the cosmos in the service of a noble cause and a young damsel. Even though the game is pretend, his Great Evaluator is patting him on the back. He's having fun and the pretending makes him feel good. Dinner, on the other hand, is a low self-esteem activity for Jeff because his father always grills him about school, and school is not his strong suit. The lesson here? *Kids switch easily from low self-esteem activities to high ones, but not the other way around.* If Dad understood this, he might approach the problem of his son's nutrition differently and find a better way to get him in for dinner (as well as not question him about school).

At other times understanding self-esteem may permit a parent to avoid negative judgments about a child's normal reactions. Katie, for example, is thirteen and she is upset that her best friend scored better than she did on their school achievement tests.

> Katie: Janelle beat me on the Iowas. I'll bet she's
>   loving it. Creep!
> Parent: Listen, dear, everyone is good at something
>   and not so good at something.
> Katie: Yeah, well looks like I'm the stinkpot in this

one, doesn't it?

Parent: You shouldn't compare yourself to other
children, anyway. What matters is what you think
and how you're doing yourself, not what everybody
else is doing.

Katie: Well, what I think is I'm stupid. So I guess
that's what matters, right?

Parent: That's not what I'm saying.

Katie: Just drop it, will ya?

Katie's Great Evaluator is comparing her to another student, not liking the result and letting her know about it in no uncertain terms. The lesson? *Kids are very competitive.* Even though it's skewed, Katie's competitive reaction is normal. After this conversation with her parent, however, she's likely to go off sullen and confused. In addition to her competitive problem, she now feels worse because she has been told her reaction was out of line.

Understanding self-esteem also helps you relax sometimes, because you realize you can't do everything for your children or protect them from all attacks on their egos. When parents overidentify with their children, they tend to feel the child's emotional upset as if it were their own. In fact, parents often feel much more upset and for a longer period of time than their children do. Imagine this scene:

Chris: Those guys won't let me play soccer with them.

Dad: Why not?!

Chris: They said I'm too little and I'm no good. I am
not! I could beat them!

Dad: Well that's the last straw!! I'm sick and tired of
those kids pushing everybody else around. You
come out there with me and we'll see whether or not
you can play with them!

Dad storms out of the house with Chris in tow and proceeds to make the situation worse. Dad couldn't stand the thought of *his* Chris being rejected, just as he couldn't handle rejection very well when he was in high school. Five hours later he lies awake in bed, still fuming, while Chris is sleeping peacefully, having forgotten the whole thing.

Let's redo this catastrophe:

> Chris: Those guys won't let me play soccer with them.
> Dad: Why not?
> Chris: They said I'm too little and I'm no good. I am
>   not! I could beat them!
> Dad: You probably could. That's too bad.
> Chris: What a bunch of jerks! I don't want to play with
>   them anyway!
> Dad: I think you're right.

Here Dad just patiently listens. He doesn't get all upset himself or go out and try to persuade the big fellows to let Chris join their game. In the midst of the "crisis" he also doesn't try to tell his son what to do or how to think. Parenting just became a lot easier.

So, if you're going to help your children develop self-esteem you need to understand the problem from the child's perspective—not yours. Keep in mind the following points about the nuts and bolts of self-esteem:

1. Self-esteem—proving yourself and growing up—is like a full-time job to children. To them it means fun as well as pressure.
2. Self-esteem for kids involves many tasks—getting along with others, doing well in school, looks and physical skills, and putting forth effort and behaving. It's complex and revolutionary.
3. Your children are going to do most of this work themselves without your help. You are not running their show, but you'll help where you can.
4. Self-esteem depends upon how others are doing relative to your kids and how they are doing relative to their own past performances. Both count.
5. Self-esteem depends both on how children evaluate themselves and how others evaluate them, but they

carry inside them their own final judge.

6. The child's Great Evaluator is a mixed blessing. He helps motivate, but he also exaggerates both pride and embarrassment.

Parental Self-Control and the Great Evaluator

When treated properly, the Great Evaluator inside your child can be a very positive force for producing success and good self-esteem. You should think of yourself and the Evaluator as a kind of team whose job is to encourage, motivate and teach your youngster the skills that will help her get along well with other people, become competent and independent, manage her physical self and develop a strong character.

To do this you must remember how the Evaluator works. He can be a bit like a loose cannon: if you don't control your own emotions, he will get worse. Easily impressed by significant others, repetition and strong emotion, he is a powerful force inside your child—totally separate from you—that pushes the child to succeed. You automatically qualify as a significant other, though, so what you repeat and what emotions you show in relation to your child will be important.

The Evaluator also is prone to exaggeration and overgeneralization, and these are qualities that you must be careful with. Kids say to themselves things like "I'm an idiot!," "I'm great!," "I'm always screwing up!," and "I'm totally awesome!" (They say the same things to other children in the beginning.) You do not want to consistently exaggerate either your child's strengths or her weaknesses. If you overdo the compliments, you run the risk of losing your credibility with your child, especially after she is about eight-years-old or so. At about that age, she is beginning to be able to discern the difference between arbitrary praise and real success. She is learning what the rules and standards are.

Unfortunately, if you overdo the negative feedback, the exact reverse does not apply. *Consistent negative feedback is usually expressed with a strong emotion: anger.* As we saw before, the negative also has a natural advantage because man is a problem-solving, problem-oriented animal. Kids, therefore, have a hard time separating inaccurate, emotional criticism from reality. Instead their Great Evaluator—who is not smart anyway—tends to identify the child with the feedback. After all, it comes from an important person, it is repeated and it comes with strong feeling.

Just as repeated criticism can damage self-esteem, so can repeated anxiety. *Overly anxious parents worry so much about the child's making a mistake that they don't let her practice and learn needed skills.* You can't dress yourself because the colors might not match and you'll look silly (and I'll look like I'm not a good mother). Don't get on the bike because you might fall over and break your arm. Don't sleep over at a friend's house because you might get homesick and who knows what your friend's parents are really like in the first place.

The self-esteem of kids who are held back in this way suffers in three ways. First, they don't develop the satisfaction that comes with reasonable independence. Second, someone telling you how nervous they are about what you are going to do represents *the opposite of a vote of confidence.* They are really saying, "You probably can't handle this yourself and so I'm justifiably worried about you." Although it may not appear hostile or abusive, this will be experienced as a direct attack on self-esteem. The Great Evaluator is sure to take this kind of criticism to heart. Too much parental anxiety strikes at the very center of the child's sense of competence.

Third, a basic law of parenting is "Anxious parent/Angry kid." A parent who is consistently overanxious about his child's behavior *and who consistently verbalizes this anxiety to the child* is going to make that youngster real mad. And when kids get consistently mad at their parents, they tend to feel guilty and their self-esteem drops.

Basically, then, working with the child's Great Evaluator means parents must learn to control their own fight-or-flight response. Too much anger or too much anxiety are serious threats to any child's self-esteem.

11

Effective Discipline

Good parenting involves both promoting self-esteem in kids and teaching them self-discipline. For kids to grow up healthy, they need warmth and encouragement as well as limits and guidance. As we have seen, for parents and teachers this means a lot of hard work and a lot of straight thinking. It also often requires a difficult emotional juggling act. One minute you must be comforting, the next minute firm. One minute you must be enthusiastic and reassuring, the next minute you must say "No" and stick to your guns. These paradoxical positions feel different with a five-year-old than with a teenager, so parents need to be ready to change as their children change.

In this chapter we'll discuss the fundamental principles of the discipline side of the parenting equation. For specific discipline strategies, parents are referred to two other books: *1-2-3 Magic: Effective Discipline for Children 2-12*, and *Surviving Your Adolescents: How to Manage and Let Go Of Your 13-18 Year Olds*. Over the years parents have found these two books very helpful in providing down-to-earth, "what-to-do" approaches for managing the younger kids as well as the teenage crowd.

The Interaction of Discipline and Self-Esteem Strategies

Good discipline tactics and good self-esteem strategies depend on and reinforce each other. On the one hand, *it is very difficult to raise the self-esteem of a child you simply don't like*. The more time she spends irritating you, the more you are going to give her negative feedback and the more emotional your communications are going to be. Since you are an important person to her, your strong and repeated negative messages are going to hit her where she lives: right in the Great Evaluator. Her self-concept will become more and more negative.

How do you prevent kids from irritating you constantly? The answer is simple, but not easy: good discipline. You need specific tactics, such as those in *1-2-3 Magic*, to keep to a minimum things like arguing, fighting, screaming, teasing, pouting and tantrums. In part, this is so you can simply like your children. If you can like them—most of the time, anyway—you will then be emotionally able to do the things that nurture self-esteem, such as positive reinforcement and listening. There's no way you'll do that if you're constantly exasperated.

On the other hand, self-esteem strategies also reinforce discipline. Promoting self-esteem in children through things like shared fun and affection also promotes what is often called "bonding" between parent and child. *Bonding makes the child value the relationship more, which makes discipline easier*. A child who likes her parent is more likely to be willing to accept from that parent the more frustrating discipline side of the relationship. Bonding makes it a little easier for the child to accept those times when the parent says "No," or when it's time for bed or homework or dinner. Bonding can also make it more difficult for a parent to firmly enforce rules with a child she is exceptionally fond of, so she needs to remind herself that discipline is in the best interests of her offspring.

Goals of Discipline

The *first goal of good discipline is self-control*, or what you might think of as frustration tolerance. Good discipline fosters success in all of the self-esteem domains, but it is perhaps most helpful in regard to character.

Research has clearly shown that parents who expect something from their children tend to produce kids who are more successful and who therefore think more of themselves. In providing the discipline side of the parenting job, *Mom and Dad are required to frustrate their children on a regular basis.* This statement may sound odd to some people, but there is really nothing unusual about it. Parents must ask their kids—time and again—to do things the kids don't want to do. Go to bed, get out of bed, go to school, come home from school on time, practice your guitar, eat your spinach.

Discipline also requires that parents insist on their kids not doing things that the children often may want to do. Don't hit your sister, don't go out and play, don't eat another piece of candy, don't run into the street, don't shout in the restaurant.

The goal of this training is frustration tolerance, or self-control—a large part of character. Kids don't like restrictions, and probably never will. When discipline is handled properly by parents, however, children eventually learn not only to tolerate rules, limits and restrictions, but also to apply them to their own behavior themselves. They discover a basic principle of self-discipline: *forgoing a short-term reward in the interest of achieving a long-term goal.* If I study two hours tonight instead of watching TV, I may get an A or B on the math test tomorrow. If I don't slug my sister, I'll be able to stay up and finish watching this movie. If I run three miles a day and skip the chocolate, I may lose the weight I want by summertime so I can squeeze into that swimming suit.

Self-control also helps an individual get along with other people. For example, if I can keep my mouth shut at times, I will be a good listener and I won't blurt out insulting remarks just because they go through my mind. Self-control also helps me develop that part of character that has to do with moral integrity, including the ability to follow reasonable rules, to be honest and to be concerned about others.

A second goal of good discipline—but one that is less obvious than the first—is to *help a child develop the ability to manage negative feedback and failure.* Even when you are a young child, life does not provide you with endless praise and success. Two of the extremely important aspects of the character dimension of self-esteem are a person's ability to 1) constructively respond to negative feedback and 2) rebound from failure.

Parental discipline requires that parents frequently tell their children when they are out of line or not doing well. When done properly, the child's self-esteem is not shattered by receiving the corrective message. Consider the difference between the following two statements:

1. "Most of the time you handle things very well, but I have to tell you that you made a mistake here."
2. "You idiot! What reason could you possibly have had for doing such a stupid thing?!"

In the first case, the child knows that while she is still respected as being moral andcompetent, it is time to honestly confront an error she made. This is essentially the basis of the "counting" procedure in *1-2-3 Magic*. "That's 1" means "I'm informing you that you're out of line and it's time to shape up. In no way am I saying or implying that you are a bad or unworthy person, or that what you are doing is terrible."

The second statement above, however, directly attacks the child's competence as well as her character. It implies the child must have been either pretty dumb—or morally inept— to have done what she did. Two self-esteem dimensions are assaulted. Repeat that kind of remark—with its powerful emotion—often enough and it's sure to be incorporated by the Great Evaluator into the youngster's self-esteem package.

Good discipline does not mean that parents can't get angry at their kids when they act up. It does mean, though, that negative feedback is given to kids in such a way that it:

1. clearly points out what was done wrong
2. does not attack the child's competence or character
3. offers an efficient way of remedying the problem
4. says or implies that the parent/child relationship is still intact

When kids grow up under this kind of regime, they begin to realize that *parental disapproval—or the disapproval of others—is not the end of the world*. They also begin to learn that negative feedback can be a source of positive change for them. If the parent's information is accurate, it can provide helpful advice that leads to constructive growth. Because the children are not totally de-motivated by the feedback, they may be willing to expend the effort necessary to improve their ways of managing similar problems.

When kids grow up with overdone criticism that attacks them personally, they learn to become angry and defensive on the outside, but they feel devastated and put down on the inside. They therefore block out the message given to them, eliminating the chance to improve their behavior. Effort here is wasted on defense rather than used on growth. The angry medium has obliterated the corrective message.

Two goals of discipline—self-control and the ability to manage negative feedback—are critical to successful functioning in adulthood and the continued building and maintenance of self-esteem.

Realistic Expectations

Another basic principle of good discipline requires that parents, teachers and other caretakers have realistic expectations of what children are capable of doing and accomplishing. It is obviously going to be crippling to self-esteem if the child is not ready to do all the things the parents expect. You don't try to toilet train a twelve-month-old, expect a four-year-old to know his multiplication tables, hope that your seven-year-old son and his four-year-old sister will stop fighting for good, or punish your three-year-old daughter because she can't clean up her messy room.

Developmentally inappropriate expectations like these are frequent problems. Parents also need to be aware, however, of some other common, *unrealistic* expectations that can frequently cause trouble.

Here are a few:

Kids are naturally cooperative and unselfish. False! The younger they are, the more selfish children are. The cute little peanuts are primarily out for themselves, and they don't like it when you cross them. When they get what they want they are fun, affectionate and delightful. When they don't get what they want, crying, screaming, whining and tantrums can be the order of the day. Don't hold it against them—that's just the way little kids are.

Kids are basically rational. False! Kids in the beginning are more emotional and less rational. They are not little adults, but they have tremendous potential. Their ability to reason develops slowly, though aggressively. Often when they're little (and often when they're teens, too), even five rational explanations won't get the job done in a frustrating situation.

I should only have to tell them once. Not! Discipline means training, and training means repetition. What they're learning has an intellectual aspect to it, but it also involves increasing the emotional skill of tolerating frustration. Kids get the message when you've taught them over and over.

Parents must be realistic about the job they have. In addition to having fun with their children, feeding them and being affectionate, parents must aggravate their kids on regular basis because that's part of the job. Some kids tolerate aggravation better than others, because children have varied inborn temperaments. Few say thank you, however, or show appreciation for their parents' work and effort. Many try to test and manipulate using badgering, temper, threats and martyrdom. These actions do not indicate psychopathic personalities in the making. They are just a normal part of being a kid, and having to manage them is a normal part of being a parent.

How to Do It

Understanding the goals of discipline and knowing what to realistically expect from kids is a start. Another job is knowing exactly how to manage the problems they throw at you. The basic principle here is: don't be spontaneous—don't shoot from the hip in a crisis. Take a deep breath, put on your thinking cap for a few seconds, and keep these thoughts in mind:

1. What discipline strategies does this problem call for?
2. How do I minimize talk and emotion during discipline?
3. How do I avoid a war?

Imagine you have three children, ages nine, seven and four. One day over coffee a sympathetic visitor to your home asks you a question: "What are the three biggest problems you have with your kids?" After thinking for a few seconds, you reply: "Bedtime, teasing, and homework." If the friend then asked you how you handle these, what would your response be?

1. "I don't know, they just drive me nuts!"
2. "I do whatever comes to mind at the time."
3. "I've tried everything and nothing works."
4. "I consider running away from home."

Any one of the above, obviously, would be a sign of poor discipline. It would also mean there is probably a lot of arguing and yelling going on around the house, which does nothing for anyone's self-esteem.

Now imagine your response is different. You say, "Well, we use the Basic Bedtime Method from *1-2-3 Magic* and we use counting for teasing and sibling rivalry. For homework we use a kitchen timer, charting, and the Rough Checkout and PNP method combined with an assignment sheet." Your friend would probably fall off her chair. But more important, your home would be a much more peaceful, organized and pleasant place to live. Everyone's self-esteem would be a little higher.

Eight years later, let's imagine your friend returns and asks you the same question about your three biggest problems. You say there are now four: arguing, sibling rivalry, chores and messes around the house. She asks what you do about them, and you say, "For arguing I listen first, then state my case and then—if necessary—use the 'This conversation is stupid, I'm history' routine. For sibling rivalry we're trying negotiation like it's described in *Surviving Your Adolescents*. For chores and messes we're using the docking system and the garbage bag method, and that cuts down the hassle a lot."

You win the award for persistent valor under fire.

Talk, Emotion and War

One of the most overlooked principles of discipline is this: *no discipline will ever be effective while there's a war going on.* This means that when the anger between a parent and a child exceeds a critical level, all the tactics in the world—rewards, punishments, groundings, fines, chores—

become irrelevant. Why? Because when anger hits a certain level a person's goal changes from being rational to being emotional and irrational. What I now want is to win at all costs. I want to hurt someone. I want not to lose. I want to save face. I want revenge.

Punishments such as groundings, fines and chores can be very effective parts of discipline. So can rewards. But often discussions of punishment in child-rearing books use examples where the punishment is either physical or it is accompanied by excessive parental anger or just plain rage. Then the book goes on to say that punishment is ineffective. Of course that kind of punishment is ineffective, because it's changing the whole nature of the game. It's starting a war.

Some wars start when parents inadvertently dump their own frustrations on their kids. Kids' irritating behavior triggers their parents' anger about their own own work, marriage, aging, health or self-esteem. This is often referred to as displacement, or emotional dumping, and it's a constant threat.

Other wars start with innocent attempts on the part of parents to explain discipline to their children, especially when the kids resist it. If one explanation works, fine. But once an argument begins, the conversation can become irrational, and it may progress through what we call the "Talk-Persuade-Argue-Yell-Hit" syndrome. At the end of this we have war again, and any chances for rational discipline are lost.

When parents say, "We tried that tactic and it didn't work," often the answer is, "Of course it didn't work. There's been a war going on at your house for the last four years."

Testing and Manipulation

A final important and often overlooked part of discipline has to do with managing children's reactions to discipline. Too many people think the job is done once they have come up with a discipline tactic for a particular problem. On the contrary, that's just the first half of the job.

When kids are being disciplined, they are usually frustrated. They have two choices for dealing with this frustration. They can accept it— grudgingly or gracefully—and do what they're supposed to do. When parents are kind, warm and reasonable in what they are asking, their attitude helps the child learn self-control and frustration tolerance. This is a kind of emotional skill that builds gradually over the years.

The child's second choice for dealing with the frustration, however, is to fight it by getting into some kind of testing and manipulation. Through these tactics, children try to get their way, avoid discipline and get their parents off track. Readers of *1-2-3 Magic* and *Surviving Your Adolescents* are very familiar with the six kinds of testing and manipulation:

1. Badgering
2. Temper
3. Threats
4. Martyrdom
5. Butter-up
6. Physical

Most of these tactics are "designed" to make the parent feel uncomfortable enough to drop whatever attempt he was making at training his child. In fact, most children will immediately drop the testing tactic as soon as they get what they want.

As we saw before, "permissive" parents are more vulnerable to testing and manipulation. They often take testing as a sign that their kids are experiencing some intolerable kind of pain, and they try to rid their youngsters of it as soon as possible by giving them what they want. Discipline here, therefore, doesn't really exist, and the notion of frustration tolerance becomes more and more foreign to these children. They get what they want today and—without knowing it—sacrifice their long-term successes.

In addition to getting their way, these children have also successfully learned how to obliterate negative feedback, rather than learning from it. Instead of mastering self-control, they have mastered "other-control" through manipulation. The risk is that these children will grow up to be immature, dependent, demanding and offensive.

The Comfort of Limits

True or False? Self-esteem and creativity both are higher when kids can "do their own thing" without external limits imposed by adult power or authority. Believe it or not, this statement is false. A number of studies have come up with the conclusion—which makes sense when you think about it—that kids feel better about themselves and perform better, creatively and otherwise, when they learn the boundaries for reasonable behavior.

The world itself has all kinds of limits and rules. There are rules for how to treat other people, speed limits, laws about property rights, rules for sports, interest payments, taxes and marriage. You may not like all these regulations, but *if you don't recognize them, you will get hurt* and wind up more frustrated than you would be if you followed them. Parents are the ones who introduce their children to life's boundaries.

How parents establish rules and set limits—or fail to set limits—not only has a tremendous effect on the self-esteem of a child, but also affects the relationship between parent and child, the parent's own self-esteem and the overall atmosphere for everyone around the home. These effects are long-lasting.

The parents' job here is also complicated. First it involves coming up with reasonable rules. Next these rules must be communicated clearly to the children. Finally, they must be enforced on a regular basis in the face of frequent testing and manipulation.

You frequently hear the phrase, "Believe it or not, kids really want limits." This isn't quite the case. It is true that in the long run, children are more comfortable in a house where parents have clear, reasonable rules and enforce them consistently and fairly. The kids are more comfortable whether or not they realize the connection. At any one moment, however, kids want what they want, and they are angry and disappointed if they don't get it. This often leads to testing and manipulation.

The bottom line: *if kids are successful in their testing efforts, they will continue to use these tactics in the future*. The household will suffer the consequences: prolonged and frequent periods of emotional upset. Our own research has revealed that kids' favorite tactics are Badgering, Temper and Martyrdom, and none of these make for peace and enjoyable relationships. When children use these kinds of testing regularly, however, everyone's self-esteem takes a beating.

Imagine two three-and-a-half-year-olds, Joe and Ben, in two different homes. Both children want Sugar Crisp cereal for breakfast, and their parents get it for them. Both children then change their minds when the bowl arrives and demand Frosted Flakes instead. The parents, naturally, resist, saying, "No dear, this is what you wanted," which prompts the children to knock the bowl of cereal on the floor and go into a major fit of temper. They scream at the top of their lungs, become beet-red, and pound the table with both hands.

A defining moment for the future of parents and children alike. Joe's mother calmly counts. "That's 1." She knows children get like this sometimes, and though it's very aggravating, he's just a kid. In spite of the counting, Joe continues his tantrum. After the third count, Mom escorts Joe—still yelling—to his room for a short rest period.

Ben's father, on the other hand, becomes very upset and first tries to be firm with his son. He can't stand this kind of conflict and doesn't know why the kid has to be so unreasonable. He explains that Ben must eat what he requested and he can't go around throwing his food on the floor. Ben howls louder. His father now pleads, "Come on now, this is ridiculous," as he glances nervously at the clock. They must leave for preschool and the train in seven minutes. "All right, all right, just shut up! Here's your stupid cereal and you'd better eat it all, pal!" Ben chows down happily.

Upon visiting the two households a year and a half later, we find that five year old Joe is learning "HFT"—high frustration tolerance—which will be an important part of his character. He is better, though far from perfect, at tolerating his parents' No's because their limits are also fair and reasonable and he knows they mean business. The home is generally peaceful, and Joe often spends time reading with his parents. He's learning to recognize quite a few letters and words.

When we enter Ben's house, however, we are greeted with screaming. It's Ben vs. Mom this time. The child never seems to be able to take No for an answer! Ben is learning "LFT"—low frustration tolerance. His temper is terrible, and often Mom and Dad just give him what he wants to avoid a battle. At other times, though, they don't feel he should be running the house, so they make periodic efforts to "outscream" him. Lately this has resulted in his hitting them, and then—totally fed up—they spank him and put him in his room. Their reaction leaves them feeling terribly guilty. They used to try to read to him on occasion, but quit because he was so temperamental. Now for the most part they try to avoid interaction with him unless it's absolutely necessary.

Fantasy? Not at all. Limits—properly explained, imposed and enforced—have a dramatic effect on the comfort level around the house. They allow affection to unfold naturally and learning to take place. They also produce an atmosphere where other things that foster self-esteem can occur: positive reinforcement, listening and fun.

As Joe gets older, his parents will want to gradually evolve in their discipline from dictatorship (at age 5) to "almost democracy" (around age 17). For example, as Joe develops his own internal judge (the third self-esteem revolution), Mom and Dad will want to begin to negotiate more when there are problems. Many parents find that regular family meetings are helpful and increase their children's self-esteem because the children become active participants in the problem solving process around the house. As the children hit the teen years, parents also must learn to "let go" more and more, allowing their adolescents greater freedom to manage their own affairs in such areas as money, appearance, friends, room cleanings (or absence of room cleanings), homework and use of the phone. As a child, increasing your level of independence—competently—is a wonderful boost to self-esteem.

12

Positive and Negative Feedback

A large part of parenting involves letting children know when they're on-target and when they're off-base. There is an art to providing positive, as well as negative, feedback to children. "Positive reinforcement" refers to the praise and verbal encouragement that adults give to kids. The hardest thing about praise is remembering to give it as the children get older. When they are little, cute and cuddly, it's easy to babble all day about how wonderful they are. As they get older (when they're entering junior high, for example), it often seems they're "just kids," so parents have a tendency to feel their children don't need as much attention. Other younger siblings may occupy more of Mom and Dad's time.

The third primary self-esteem revolution is the appearance of the Great Evaluator at about age eight. He needs to be worked with, and he *will* be, one way or another. Children judge themselves as soon as they can think about themselves, and their self-concept is easily swayed in the beginning by words from important adults—parents and teachers. Messages that are repeated and that contain strong feelings will be remembered by the Evaluator and repeated to the child when the adults are not around.

Honesty, Tailoring and Emotion

Though praising children may seem to be a pretty straightforward business, it is essential to be honest, tailor praise to the child and express your feelings clearly.

Preschoolers thrive on enthusiastic praise from their parents. How honest does it have to be? Not very. Four year old Johnny picks up a football which isn't much smaller than he is. He drops it, kicks it all of four feet, then trips. His NFL career is already in jeopardy.

"Johnny, what a good kick!" cooes his adoring mother. "That was wonderful. What a strong boy you are."

Johnny beams with pride and takes another energetic whack at the ball. He doesn't have much of an idea what is going on, but he does know he made that ball move and that his mother is proud of him. At the moment he's not comparing his "performance" to anybody else's, or to that of the Dallas Cowboys' punter.

Preschoolers can often be praised arbitrarily, regardless of how well they have actually done. It's most important that they tried and had fun, because they are learning and changing so rapidly. Their self-esteem is constantly on a high. The self-esteem revolution that produces the true Great Evaluator inside them has not taken place yet.

Once kids hit school, however, honesty and accuracy become more important. Kids can—and should be—reinforced for trying, but they should also be given honest and accurate feedback that is more related to what they really do. As Bill Damon mentions in *Greater Expectations*, at this age kids are intensely focused on how they are doing and what they are like. They will become quite suspicious of constant, exuberant praise.

At this point, parents and teachers also need to think about "tailoring" feedback to children according to how the child can best receive it. Some kids like rather syrupy praise, while others prefer a more businesslike manner. The goal is to praise the child, not to embarrass him.

Melissa, nine years old, comes running home from school with a 100% on her spelling test for the week. Dad says, "Why Melissa, that's fantastic! I can't believe it! You got every single one right!! We're going to call Mommy at the office, put it on the refrigerator, and fax it to Grandma in Florida!"

Melissa is delighted. Her older brother, Steve, however, who is twelve, would get nauseated with that kind of treatment. For him "Good job, Son, keep up the good work" and a pat on the back are enough.

Positive reinforcement also has a lot to do with how a parent or teacher is feeling. Adults don't give out much praise when they are not feeling good themselves. An angry or depressed adult is more inclined to say nothing or to criticize. The moral of the story is obvious, but easier said than done. First of all, sometimes you have to force yourself to say something, even though you don't much feel like it. Second, children's self-esteem will be affected by the overall emotional welfare of the adults who care for them.

Building a Self-Concept

Parents and teachers can play an active role in helping the child and her Evaluator produce and evaluate her self-concept. Praise can play a large role in this, but it should be given with an awareness of how self-esteem operates. As we discussed earlier, self-esteem becomes revolutionized in the primary grades, children's self-concepts actually develop different, intertwined parts that are based on the interpersonal, competence, physical and character dimensions.

In giving children feedback that builds self-esteem, three factors should be kept in mind:

> 1. Praise should include, at different times, *all four dimensions* of the child's life.
> 2. Praise should repeatedly identify and reinforce a child's *real strengths* in each dimension.
> 3. Positive reinforcement should be done at times *in front of an "audience."*

Remember that children, more so than adults, are faced with dealing with all four domains of their existence. They can't choose, for example, not to go to gym class or not to do their homework. As they get older, they become more and more reflective and more often attempt to come up with judgments of global esteem. We have seen before, however, that the scanning process a person uses to evaluate overall competence or worth can be erratic or incomplete. It can become too focused on negative areas that are perceived as weak or as involving unfinished business.

Adults need to help children scan accurately and thoroughly. By giving feedback in all four self-esteem areas, adults can help a child build a self-concept that is comprehensive and not oversimplified. The child can stay focused on her strengths in each dimension, though parental feedback may also—as we'll see later—involve some corrective suggestions. Parents should use what we call the "sandwich" or "positive-negative-positive" format. The positive comment comes first, then negative feedback is given if it is absolutely necessary, then the "session" is concluded with another positive comment.

Kids will remember what is repeated to them about themselves from significant adults. It is important that what is repeated to the child be positive and accurate; for most kids it is not difficult to find good things to comment on. The child's Great Evaluator will then be more inclined to incorporate these messages in the self-judgment process. Otherwise, you never quite know what the Evaluator will use as grist for the mill. Kids are prone to amazing negative distortions, which—without regular adult feedback—can go unnoticed and unchecked.

Mike, for example, is eleven. When playing with other children, he is willing to share his things and is quite comfortable getting on the phone to find someone to play with. In his schoolwork he is especially good at math and is very neat. In physical activities he is a little uncoordinated, but extremely competitive. As far as character goes, he always seems to try hard and is sensitive to the feelings of both children and adults.

Mike's parents' have observed these good qualities, and they want to be certain he's aware of them as well. Their positive reinforcement to him, therefore, includes the following statements about real strengths:

Social:

  "I like to see you sharing your things with your friends."
  "You don't need me to handle your social life. You sure know
    how to get the ball rolling!"

Competence:

> "At the conference your teacher told us your math homework is
> always excellent."
> "I can see how careful you were in doing this paper."

Physical:

> "You're a pretty big guy. If I'm one of those players on the other
> soccer team, I'm going to get out of the way when you're
> coming!"

Character:

> "Your Dad and I really like the amount of effort you're putting
> into your schoolwork."
> "It was very kind of you to talk to your Aunt Sally for so long.
> I know she enjoyed it, even though you looked like you were
> getting a little tired!"

Mike's parents also mention these things to other people when Mike
is around, as well as when he isn't. This is capitalizing on the "audience"
effect: *self-esteem is enhanced when admirable qualities or deeds are
appreciated by more people.* So Mom and Dad can mention these things
in front of Uncle Bill or at the dinner table at Thanksgiving (the message
still must be tailored to the child and it must be accurate). Teachers can use
the same strategy in the classroom to reinforce good behavior or hard
work. Here the entire class is the audience.

These messages need to be repeated, in different ways, so Mike will
get the idea. He will also be coming up with his own thoughts. His ultimate
self-concept will be a combination of his Great Evaluator's judgments of
himself, his parents' evaluations and the opinions of other people. If the
whole process of self-concept is simply left up to the Evaluator, there is
more danger that self-esteem will be skewed. In the physical realm, for
example, Mike might begin to focus more on his lack of coordination than
on his size or competitiveness.

Notice, also, that Mike's parents' comments praise him for things
that are matters of luck (his size) as well as things over which he has

control (the amount of labor he puts into his homework). Both are part of self-concept and thus have an important effect on self-esteem.

So from time to time Mike's parents continue to tell their son how they think he's doing. They are honest and they cover all areas. They are also aware of the fact that Mike will soon be making the difficult junior high transition, and they want to help make sure he has some stable and positive self-concepts to take with him. They do this in spite of the fact that Mike has a charming little eighteen-month-old sister who takes up a lot of their time and attention!

Don't Forget Character

"It's not whether you win or lose, it's how you play the game" is one of the most famous half-lies of all time. At the other extreme is its opposite, another well-known untruth, "Winning is the only thing." People can get very emotional and quite confused when discussing these statements.

The truth is, winning is important. That's W-I-N-N-I-N-G. It's fun and it feels good. It boosts self-esteem. Beating—or being better than—someone else or some other team can be one of life's great highs, especially with a nice, big audience. In certain situations, however, manners and politics require that you admit to enjoying winning only very carefully and properly.

How you play the game—sports or life itself—is also important. Character is important to success, and it *should be* important to self-esteem. By character I mean: 1) integrity—your ability to adhere to certain values, 2) effort—the mental and physical energy you expend, 3) courage—the ability to do something in spite of being afraid, and 4) kindness—the concern you show for others.

One might expect that character and self-esteem would be closely connected. These days, however, the link appears to be weak and erratic. Integrity, for example, is often taken for granted. Effort and courage may, in fact, be disconnected entirely from self-respect, and concern for others, which might build self-esteem, is often not acted upon.

People who generally follow the rules simply assume compliance is normal, and therefore their actions do not contribute to their self-esteem. The problem occurs when integrity is put to the test. If an individual gives in to temptation, her self-esteem suffers. If she does not give in to temptation, she may simply feel she just dodged a bullet and breathe a sigh of relief instead of giving herself a pat on the back. In our society today, therefore, it seems that integrity is only connected to the Great Evaluator in a negative way. It may be admired in other people, but not in oneself. Do the right thing, you take it for granted. Do the wrong thing, you criticize yourself.

Other parts of character, effort and courage, appear to be *totally separated* from the Evaluator's awareness. People who suffer from different kinds of anxiety, for example, often commit many acts of bravery every day, from showing up for work, to making phone calls, to dealing face to face with people who intimidate them. As a rule they do not, however, give themselves an ounce of credit for bravery. On the contrary, they still feel cowardly and their self-esteem is continually pounded because they feel anxious. They do not judge themselves on their behavior, they judge themselves on their feelings.

People who put in a tremendous amount of effort only feel good if the effort is successful. If they win the game or produce a great product, they can sometimes congratulate themselves for both the effort and the results. It certainly is important to win or to be successful. But if someone loses the game or the fruit of his labor is not acceptable, no credit is felt for anything.

Finally, many people feel good about themselves when they do something helpful for other people. They feel better if their act is recognized and appreciated, but they can still feel good to some extent even if it isn't. It seems, however, that today people think to do this kind of thing less and less, thus losing access to a natural self-esteem builder.

You do not want your children to think and feel this way. You want them to feel pride in their courage, effort and kindness. Why? Two reasons. First of all, it certainly seems logical to consider courage, effort and kindness as admirable qualities. They should be hooked up with the Evaluator in each person. Second, long-run success in the other self-esteem domains—interpersonal, competence and physical—often depends on integrity, courage, persistent effort and helpfulness to others.

The job of parents and teachers here is to help reconnect the Great

Evaluator to the character dimension. This is part of Damon's message in *Greater Expectations*. The judge inside each child must learn to evaluate the youngster's behavior in terms of its goodness or badness. Children also need to learn to feel better about themselves when they do something in spite of being afraid, or when they spend their last ounce of mental and physical energy for a good cause.

Positive reinforcement can play a role here in putting these critical personal qualities back in the self-esteem picture where they belong, without reverting to the half-lies and silly platitudes that children see right through. Consider the following:

> "Your paper was great, and I especially like the way
> you stuck with it there in the beginning when
> things were going terribly."
>
> "You know something? I think I know how you feel
> about school these days, and I give you a lot of credit
> for just showing up. Takes a lot of guts."
>
> "I didn't like what I found out, but I'm glad you told
> me the truth about what happened."
>
> "You were more scared than a soldier going into
> battle, but you went and gave the speech. That's the
> way to do it!"
>
> "I feel awful you guys lost. It may not be any consola-
> tion, but we all admired you for playing your hearts
> out right till the end."
>
> "You could've gone along with the rest of them and
> you didn't. If I were you I'd give myself a big pat on
> the back, because it's for sure that nobody else is
> going to."

Giving Negative Feedback

Unfortunately, parenting doesn't always involve assessing a child's strengths and giving positive feedback. There are plenty of times when you must point out something that is a weakness, mistake or fault. Doing this will inevitably lower a child's self-esteem for a period of time, which you hope is brief. Part of the character dimension that you want your kids to learn is the ability to respond well to negative feedback: being able to listen to the criticism, evaluate it, and—if it is accurate—put forth the effort to change the problem.

In the best scenario here, the Great Evaluator will be doing his job well. *The child's self-esteem will drop, which will be painful and will motivate the youngster to correct the difficulty.* When this has been done, the opportunity for praise again presents itself—both for the new behavior as well as for the effort involved in changing.

Several basic principles should be kept in mind when giving constructive criticism. First, before giving negative feedback, review in your own mind your "other concept" of the child. Chances are the child is basically a good person and doing most of what's expected of him. In the context of his overall behavior, what you are about to point out may be minor.

Second, unless it's absolutely necessary, don't give feedback when you are furious or very upset. If you do, you'll confuse the Great Evaluator, who won't be able to tell the difference between a few constructive suggestions and total condemnation. Remember that strong emotion always impresses him. A tantrum from an important person will knock the child's self-esteem right through the floor, and the message will be remembered only as "You are a rotten kid!" The other content will be lost, leaving the child with no motivation to change anything.

Third, be clear what you are talking about and discuss only one thing at a time. Keep the discussion brief. Some parents get onto the old "and while I'm at it let let me tell you a few other things" roll and bring up all the qualities they don't like about their offspring. They intended to give constructive criticism about the child's insensitivity to a friend, but wound up throwing in the messy room, the grade in reading, the roller blades on the kitchen counter and the relationship with a younger sister.

Finally, end the conversation with some encouraging comment, such as:

> "I'm sure you'll do better next time."
> "When I've told you about things I don't like before, you
>   always seem to work hard to correct the problem."

For every person on earth, part of life will be dealing with negative feedback from time to time. Inaccurate criticism can legitimately be dismissed by an objective Evaluator. Realistic negative feedback, on the other hand, should be attended to and should cause a temporary drop in self-esteem. Remember that part of your goal is to help your child master the art of accepting and learning from constructive criticism.

Healthy Demandingness

We are indebted to Baumrind and Coopersmith for giving us a major wake-up call: *parents who demand things of their kids are the ones who are really interested in the self-esteem of their children.* Neither permissiveness nor the repressive, authoritarian style has a place in raising children who have self-respect. A "healthy demandingness," combined with warmth and respect, defines the authoritative style that is most conducive to developing the two things necessary for good self-esteem: adequate performance and a fair Great Evaluator.

The notion of being "demanding" makes some parents nervous. But demands or expectations can be communicated in ways that are reasonable and motivating, rather than irrational and demotivating. Which of the following comments, in your opinion, are examples of healthy demandingness?

> "That's pretty good, but I think you can do better."
> "What is this garbage?! Can't you do better than that?"
> "It's four o'clock. Time to get that homework done."
> "Turn off that stupid TV. When are you going to get
>   started and do something for a change?"
> "You haven't missed a swimming practice for two
>   months. I like to see that kind of commitment."
> "So now, all of a sudden, you're skipping practice?
>   Your coach is going to love that!"
> "I thought you were sort of rude to Melissa."
> "You keep treating people like that, and you won't
>   have any friends left."
> "Your hair looks lovely. How did you get it like that?"

"You're not going out again looking like that, are
   you?"

"You actually asked Bob to the turnabout dance? You
   got guts, baby! Nice going!"

"What's the big problem with giving a speech on the
   Industrial Revolution? Just get up there and do it."

In summary, positive and negative feedback—honestly telling a child what she is doing right and wrong—is an important part of building a child's self-concept and self-esteem. This information needs to be repeated, because the Evaluator remembers frequent feedback from important people. Especially around age eight or so, it is important to *help a child with his first impressions of himself.* Feedback also needs to cover regularly all four dimensions of the child's life: social, competence, physical and character. Otherwise, you never quite know what the energetic Evaluator is going to come up with. Kids are prone to amazing negative distortions, and—without regular adult feedback—hidden self-prejudice can go unnoticed.

13

Listening

Many more parents today are familiar with what is often called "active listening" than was the case twenty years ago. Active listening was originally described by a psychologist, Carl Rogers, for whom the technique was the basis of his form of psychotherapy. Later another author, Haim Ginott, did an excellent job of applying the technique to children in his books, *Between Parent and Child* and *Between Parent and Teenager*.

Active listening is good for children's self-esteem for several reasons. First of all, one of the self-esteem revolutions requires that children more and more earn their self-respect. Active listening can communicate confidence in the child and her ability to handle her feelings and problems. It is inherently respectful, and coming from an important person, such as a parent or teacher, this respect helps the child more respect herself. Many times parents realize through listening that, even though their child may be upset, the child can handle things herself and the parents don't really need to do anything.

Active listening also lets kids know that their feelings are normal and nothing to be ashamed of. Though feelings can present problems, they are not in themselves right or wrong. Actions can be right or wrong. Active listening can be very comforting and supportive, especially when a child is upset. There is a kind of closeness involved for both people in the experience of listening and being listened to, which can be especially important to children during times of stress, such as entry into first grade and entry into junior high.

Finally, active listening lets a parent get to know—or stay in touch with—their child. It often provides useful information that a parent needs in order to do what must be done to further the child's welfare. Listening can be especially important during the teenage years when the kids are starting to pull away more from their parents. As we have seen, in the beginning a child's self-esteem depends a lot on parents' unconditional love. One of the major self-esteem revolutions, however, is the addition of the conditional love of other people to the self-esteem equation. Active listening is one way that children can stay connected to—and feel support from—the basic acceptance and commitment that their parents feel toward them.

The Attitude of Listening

Parents can effectively use listening in situations that are emotionally loaded as well as in those in which nothing much is happening. When active listening is done well it becomes second nature, and doesn't feel like a "tactic" or "strategy" at all. It's just a good way to talk with someone.

The first problem is remembering or thinking to do it. You might "turn the switch" in your brain to LISTEN, for example, in situations where a child is very upset, where you need more information to understand what he is thinking, or where he needs some support while he sorts a problem out.

Active listening starts with an attitude. The attitude is to understand what someone else is thinking and feeling without judging it. You can't active listen if in your mind you are evaluating what you are hearing and preparing a rebuttal to it. People—even young children—can sense this. It will affect how they feel and what they say.

Today we know that human communication is more complicated than we had previously imagined. What one person means to say is not always what another one hears. If your attitude is that you are really trying to understand what someone else is telling you, you must periodically check with him to see if you are really getting his story straight.

Sometimes the listener will give the other person a summary of what he thinks that person is saying, or perhaps reflect back the feelings that he hears being described. The person being listened to can then say if the other is on target or not. Being listened to in this way is usually a pleasant experience. It's nice to know someone understands what you're going through. *His effort shows that he considers you a valuable or worthwhile person.*

All this may make active listening sound more complicated and "shrink-like" than it really is. A few examples—of both good and bad listening—will help. Active listening can serve a number of purposes, which include diffusing emotional states, staying in touch and serving as a preliminary to negotiations with older children.

Diffusing Emotional States

Four-year-old Shannon comes in from playing with the neighbors and their new puppy. Her mother sees she's crying.

> "I want Friskie back!"
> "Oh, honey, what's the matter?"
> "We don't have a doggie anymore!" (Crawls on Mom's lap.)
> "You really miss him, don't you?" (Hugs her daughter.)
> "Yeah." (Sniffles)
> "Everybody felt bad, didn't they?"
> "Yeah...Mom?"
> "What?"
> "I'm going back outside now."
> "OK, dear."

This was good active listening. Mom also realized—or at least hoped—she didn't have to do anything other than be comforting to diffuse the emotional tension. Two hours later Shannon's outside having a wonderful time and Mom's still teary. The joys of parenting!

Bad listening in this situation? It might go like this:

> "I want Friskie back!"
> "Dear, he died six weeks ago. There's nothing I can do
>   about that. We all felt bad."
> "I don't have a doggie anymore!"
> "Neither does anyone else in this family."
> "I want a new dog! They got one—why can't I have one?"

Off to the races.

Here's another example of emotional diffusion. Tony is nine years old and participating in spring little league:

> "I don't want to go to the game tonight."
> "I thought you were pitching."
> "I was."
> "What's the matter?"
> "What if there's a tornado? The sky's green."
> "Bad weather really bothers you, doesn't it?"
> "I hate it! But I'll look stupid if I run home again in the
>   middle of the game."
> "Yeah, you were pretty embarrassed after that. What do
>   you think you're going to do?"

This is very respectful. The parent chooses not to push the youngster in the face of the strong anxiety involved. Strong anxiety tends to make people feel stupid anyway, and the boy doesn't need more put-downs. Maybe he'll decide to go. Whether he does or not, the parent here is expressing confidence in *his* ability to handle the situation.

Bad listening in tornado weather?

> "I don't want to go to the game tonight."
> "I thought you were pitching."
> "I was."
> "What's the matter?"
> "What if there's a toronado? The sky's green."
> "Don't be silly. You can't just stay home. The whole rest

of the team is depending on you."

"Let somebody else get blown away. I'm not going out
   there!"

"I'm sorry, but you have to go."

"I'M NOT GOING!!"

Emotional explosion instead of diffusion. The tornado's going to be
in the house, and everyone's self-esteem is going to suffer.

Staying in Touch

Parents of teens often find themselves agitated, one way or another, about
their growing adolescent charges. The most frequent aggravations involve
sibling rivalry and arguing, but Mom and Dad also worry about more
heavy-duty issues like sex and drug use. You can't follow your adolescent
all over the place, but sometimes you can find out—directly from them—
something about their values and how they might handle difficult situations. Good listening can help here.

"Did you hear that Amy Wiggins is pregnant?"

"Oh my goodness. She's a senior isn't she?"

"Yeah. I was like, 'Wow, I can't believe it.' I don't know
   who the guy is."

"You must have been shocked."

"I was. I don't know her that well, but like, you know,
   how could she be so careless?"

"How do you mean?"

"Well, you know, I wasn't born yesterday. She—I mean
   they—could have used something!"

"That's true. How do girls your age feel about sex and
   birth control, anyway?"

"My, aren't we curious? No, just kidding. A lot of them
   are, like, pretty careful. Some are on the pill or use
   condoms. 'Cause a lot of these guys, you know, are
   selfish jerks."

"They certainly can be."

"I think a lot of girls aren't into having sex at all. I

> mean, they don't want a kid, but also because of
> AIDS and stuff like that. I think that makes the most
> sense."
> "You really think so?"
> "Well, what do you think? What a way to finish—or
> end—your famous high school career!"
> "You got a point there, that's for sure."

After going in the other room to faint, Mom receives an award for coolness under fire. By keeping her wits about her, she learned something about her daughter which, she hopes, is a true reflection of the girl's values. If Mom had started trying to instruct or interject her own opinions too soon, she might have gotten a resistant adolescent who would have been anything but reassuring.

Preliminary to Negotiation

Jenny is twelve and her sister, Pam, is fourteen.

> "Pamela is the biggest jerk! Talk about El Dorko."
> "What happened?"
> "She using all my stuff again! I'm totally out of shampoo!
>   Wait'll she sees what I'm gonna do to her room."
> "She's really done it this time!"
> "You betcha. One homicide a la carte, coming right up."
> "Well, we'll all miss her—except for you, of course."
> "Dad!"
> "How about you and me and the prime suspect sitting
>   down and working out this 'using my things' routine?"
> "I don't know, she's got terminal stupidity."
> "Well, I'm willing to try."

Although he may be tired of it, Dad doesn't get upset or judgmental about his daughter's anger. Sibling rivalry is tedious but normal, and Dad doesn't have to make Jenny feel guilty about temporarily wanting to do in her older sister. Thus Jenny's self-esteem was not attacked, and it was reinforced by Dad's offer to help.

The bad version of the same scene:

> "Pamela is the biggest jerk! Talk about El Dorko."
>
> "What's the problem now?"
>
> "She using all my stuff again! I'm totally out of sham-
> poo!"
>
> "Well, big deal. I doubt the whole universe is out. Use
> some of mine instead of having a cow about it."
>
> "Wait'll she sees what I'm gonna do to her room."
>
> "You just watch your step, young lady."
>
> "You tell Miss Piggy to watch her step!"
>
> "I'm sick and tired of the two of you!"

When *Not* to Listen

Parents reading these examples sometimes get nervous, feeling they may be abdicating their authority and letting the kids do whatever they want. That's far from the case. The trick is to decide when it's time to listen and when it's time for something else, like setting limits. Imagine this scene. It's 11:30 PM on a Tuesday, Mom and Dad are asleep and sixteen-year-old Susan comes into the bedroom:

> "Hey, you guys, I'm going nuts with this term paper. I'm
> driving over to Bob's for a while."
>
> "You're feeling restless and need some company?"

This isn't very realistic. The correct response more likely would be, "I wish you could, but it's past midnight and school's tomorrow." Then Mom and Dad brace themselves for some good old-fashioned testing and manipulation, which won't do much for anyone's self-esteem in the short run. In the long run, however, it's better for everyone if the parents are prepared for the teen's displeasure, say what they have to say (set the limit), and don't get baited into a useless argument in the middle of the night. The conversation might go like this:

> "Hey, you guys, I'm going nuts with this term paper. I'm
> driving over to Bob's for a while."

"I wish you could, but it's real late and school's tomor-
row."
"Oh, come on, be reasonable for once."
"Sorry, but you can't go out now."
"Oh, for Pete's sake!"

The hassle is kept to a minimum, and though Susan is frustrated, she's not going to feel as bad—about life or about herself—if her parents get into a ridiculous, hostile discussion. Very likely this adolescent has learned, over the years, how to tell when Mom and Dad mean business.

14

Fun

No one should have to tell you why it's important to have fun with your kids. Or should they? To the self-esteem of a child, shared fun with a parent is extremely important. Yet it is frequently overlooked because fun itself is so simple and people are so busy. The amount of time parents spend with their kids used to be more than thirty hours per week. These days that figure has been cut in half.

Having fun with your kids, whether spontaneous or planned, ordinary or elaborate, is important for several reasons. First of all, shared fun is the glue of any good relationship. Think back to before you got married. Odds are you started dating this person because you thought he or she was a lot of fun. In fact, the purpose of dating is usually to have fun. Then you made a fateful decision: let's get married. Behind this decision—for most people—is the following logic: you're this much fun now and we're not even married. Think of how much fun we'll have when we're living together!

The problem with this thinking is that the decision to marry is usually a decision to work together—to find a place to live, maintain it, have kids and try to make as much money as you can. These activities are different from having fun. There's nothing in the world that says just because someone is fun to be with, he or she will also be a good work partner. That's why the divorce rate is around fifty per cent.

Still, fun helped cause the original bonding and affection. That's what fun does. You like someone more when you have fun with them, which also helps you get along the rest of the time. What's the most important factor for success in marriage? You always hear that it's communication. I've got news for you. The couple that plays together stays together—and stays in love.

The same is true of having fun with your children. You may like them anyway, but you'll like them more if you have fun with them on a consistent basis. And during the times when you're not having fun—when you have to provide the other side of the parenting equation, discipline— you'll find the kids are easier to deal with because you enjoyed each other's company at another time.

Anything that improves your relationship with your child will help her self-esteem. Having fun with her also sends an important message that you like her—that she is a nice and enjoyable person.

The Importance of Play

Fun is also important to your kids' self-esteem because life is work. While they're encountering all the revolutions in self-esteem as they grow up, children are striving hard to master the tasks that life presents them. For children their work and their play are often the same thing, but as kids get older, work and play become more and more different. Algebra homework is work. Going out with friends is play. Track practice is work. Running a new game on the computer is play.

Self-esteem will be influenced partly by how hard youngsters work at becoming competent in social, academic, physical and character-related aspects of their lives. And how hard people work at something often has a lot to do with their ability to take a break from it from time to time.

With all the talk about self-esteem, it's easy to forget that *what you think of yourself is not all there is to life*. Some of the most pleasant and meaningful times can occur when there is no self-evaluation going on at all. Curling up in front of a fire with a good book, finding Venus in the sky on a clear night, walking through the woods and suddenly encountering a goldfinch convention, listening to your favorite music with a friend.

You want your kids to be able to enjoy these aspects of their lives as well. You want them to appreciate some of the amazing and intriguing things the world has to offer, as well as its beautiful and peaceful features. If your children are going to have these experiences, *you need to both have fun with them and have fun without them.* Showing them that you enjoy them, but also that you have your own times for recreation, relaxation and renewal is one of the healthiest forms of modeling for both of you. No child's self-esteem is going to be helped by having a parent who is a martyr.

The "Rules"

There really aren't any "rules," for having fun, but if you want to promote self-esteem in your children there are a few guidelines.

Regularity. Whatever you do should be fairly frequent, not just the annual family vacation to Disney World. A few hours every week would put you in the exceptional-parent category right away. Remember, it's not just spending time, it's *fun* time when you are both enjoying the same thing.

Simplicity. Shared fun does not have to be elaborate or expensive. You can go out to a movie or to eat, but you can also take a walk, read a book to the littler ones, or simply take a drive in the car and talk. If they have your attention, kids can appreciate a lot of things.

Avoid martyrdom. Do something that you enjoy as well—or almost as well—as your child. If you are enjoying yourself, she'll know, she'll have a better time, and she'll feel better about herself. Keep in mind that with the little ones, you may enjoy a lot of surprising things because they allow you to relive your own childhood. Dad is still out in the sandbox making the castle long after his four-year-old has gone back in the house.

Family fun is OK, but one-on-one is best. This notion surprises a lot of people, especially those who feel that families should do everything together. That may be some parents' point of view, but the fact of the matter is that children love having one parent all to themselves. Having fun in this way is also made easier by the elimination of the eternal problem of sibling rivalry.

No problem discussions. Don't discuss problems during the fun times, unless it's absolutely necessary or the child really wants to. This is no time for you to be evaluating them. It's especially nice if they can leave their Great Evaluator home once in a while.

Your sense of humor. Almost all children appreciate and respond to humor. Unfortunately, some of them lose their own sense of humor as they get older. Laughing together is a great tonic for a lot of things.

It wouldn't be right to think of having fun with your kids as something that can only occur at a certain time and place. Fun can also be spontaneous, it can happen anywhere, and it can last for five seconds or five hours. Shooting the breeze at the dinner table or before bed, watching the new raccoon family walk across the back yard, taking a ride to the airport to pick up grandpa. Thousands of possibilities are there for the taking.

Some parents complain they don't have time for fun. Really? *Perhaps the problem isn't time, it's attitude.* Is time for yourself part of your existence as a parent, or are you dedicated to perpetual martyrdom? Shared fun is important to your children's self-esteem and to how they'll live their lives in the future. It's also one of the easiest suggestions in this book to implement.

Part IV

Think Twice

15

Common Oversights

A s we have seen, many adults are not used to looking at the problem of their children's self-esteem realistically. Because of this, there are some critical issues that are often neglected, overlooked or just plain ignored. In this chapter we will discuss seven.

1. Anxious Children

Earlier we mentioned that children's temperaments might fall into one of three categories: aggressive, normal or anxious. The aggressive children have serious social skills deficits, but, ironically, don't seem to be able to see them. The "normal" kids get along reasonably well with others and are easier to like.

It may be that the most serious self-esteem problems occur in the children who tend to be anxious, shy and withdrawn. A basic rule in psychology, is that *as anxiety goes up, self-esteem goes down*. People who are anxious are very aware of it, feel funny about it, and see others as stronger and more confident than themselves.

Shyness is especially difficult for kids. Children who are shy are often afraid that they will do the wrong thing and that others will not like them. After age eight or so, when forming same-sex peer relationships is very important, shy children become more aware of their social withdrawal and feel more frustrated by it. When they hit the teen years, the frustration of this kind of isolation can become agonizing. Unfortunately, sensitive children like this are also more reflective, and they also have more time to think about themselves and their situation because they are alone so much.

Parents often tend to forget about their shy children because these kids don't bother anyone. They are easy to overlook when you are busy with a million other things. They aren't rebellious and they are often cooperative and helpful. They don't want to offend you either. Their inner anxiety, and sometimes eventual depression, go unnoticed. To them the social dimension of their life is a big zero, and this fact drowns out whatever strengths they may have in other areas. Their Great Evaluator starts to beat on them because of this one deficiency.

What do these kids need? *They need an agent.* It may sound funny, but they need a kind of social engineer who will help them make and sustain contact with other children. Many shy kids are perfectly capable of having friends, but on their own they just can't get through the initial break-in phases of a relationship. They need a parent to pick up the phone, make the calls, invite people over, do some chaufferring and accompany them to different activities. Shy kids need exposure to other children on a regular basis.

To a young child, the difference between two friends and one friend is not such a big deal. The difference, however, between one friend and no friends is infinite.

2. Arguing Parents

A second area that is often forgotten, but which has a lot of negative impact on children's self-esteem, is parental arguing. The divorce rate still hovers around fifty per cent, and there is certainly a lot of arguing that goes on in those families before the breakup. There is often continued hostility after the split as well.

We cannot assume that everyone else who doesn't get divorced is happy. There are plenty of wars that go on continuously in families where

Mom and Dad stay together. Some of these are worse because the parents deeply resent feeling stuck with each other.

The problem with arguing in front of the children is this: *kids—especially the younger ones—always tend to assume that the problem is their fault.* That's just the way they are. It makes little difference if you tell them later that they had nothing to do with it. And a lot of the time, of course, the arguments may be specifically about the kids. Either way, the children assume they did something wrong, and often they will make sad and pathetic attempts to reconcile their warring parents. Mom and Dad, though, may be too wrapped up in hating each other and in "the principle of the thing" to appreciate the effects that their discord is having on the self-esteem of their sons and daughters.

The solution here? If you're going to argue in front of the kids, then resolve it in front of the children as well. Don't even start an argument when the children are home, unless you are prepared, emotionally and intellectually, to resolve the issue you're about to bring up.

3. Work and Self-Respect

It has been written—many times—that children need to feel that they are contributing to the family. A great way to see this happen is to make sure that they do their chores. Cleaning their rooms, taking out the garbage, feeding the dog and doing the dishes will increase their self-esteem.

Not. Anyone who knows how children think should know that this thinking is faulty. While it certainly is a good idea to encourage children to do their chores, *it is unrealistic to think that completing chores will have much impact on their self-esteem.* If they do their chores, and they have a brother who doesn't, they may get a little competitive boost and a pat on the back from Mom or Dad, but the chores themselves rarely seem to make kids feel good about themselves.

What drives parents to distraction, however, is when their children complain loudly about having to do a certain job at home. Then, if they ever do get around to it, they do a sloppy job. If the next door neighbor, however, asks them to do the same exact thing, *they will do it enthusiastically and scrupulously and feel proud of themselves afterwards!*

What kind of sense does this make? No one knows for sure, but here are two suggestions for how to play the game. If the kids have chores to do at home, the chores should be agreed upon beforehand and they should be routine. Parents should insist that the jobs be done and should praise children for doing them.

Parents should not, however, expect working around the house to boost their children's self-esteem a lot. But they should expect that working away from home *will* be a significant aid to self-esteem. This kind of work is something that should be encouraged as soon as children are old enough. They'll learn something about independence, responsibility and money management. Unfortunately, this learning may or may not transfer to the home front.

Prior to age sixteen there are things like babysitting (yes, for the boys, too), lawn mowing (yes, for the girls, too), and paper routes of different sorts. After age sixteen there is fast food! Any job is a good experience at this age. Even a bad job can teach an adolescent valuable things, such as how to handle an arrogant supervisor, manage boredom or deal with the public. These are all skills that can help provide future competence in the employment arena.

4. Television

Many adults are aware of the amazing statistic that the average child watches four to five hours of television a day. *This figure no longer shocks anyone.* We're all used to it. "What's the big deal?" people say. "Next to school, the TV is the world's best babysitter."

Ask yourself this question, however: What does television do for children's self-esteem? By age sixteen the average child will have seen 13,000 murders on TV. During a typical one-hour segment of prime-time television they will see an average of three incidents of spontaneous, romantic and unprotected sex. They will have watched thousands and thousands of commercials.

The effect on their self-esteem? Probably none. That's the point. Five hours per day multiplied by 365 days a year gives you a grand total of 1,825 hours of wasted time per year.

What else could our kids have done with those hours? They could have read, learned how to draw, mastered a new word-processing program, gone out with friends, spent time with their parents, or travelled. They could have done a better job studying for school, or have completed projects for extra credit. They could have been in the Girl Scouts or Boy Scouts, or on a soccer or swimming team. They could have been getting good at photography. They could have built a collection of coins or stamps or fossils.

They could also, after 1,825 hours, have made significant improvement playing the keyboard or piano, a skill that could give them a good deal of satisfaction for the rest of their lives.

In addition to lost learning and unrealized skills, there is another major television tragedy: *our children are getting fatter.* Since the 1960s childhood obesity has steadily increased in the United States, and eighty per cent of overweight children will continue to be overweight as adults. It is no mystery that being overweight is a grimly consistent producer of low self-esteem.

We turn to an excellent, basic text on childhood development for some startling facts. In *Infants, Children, and Adolescents*, by Laura E. Berk, we learn the following:

1. Time spent in front of the TV is the second-best predictor of future obesity among school-age children.
2. The rate of obesity *increases by two per cent for each additional hour* of TV watched per day.
3. TV time greatly reduces the time kids spend in physical exercise. At the same time, commercials encourage youngsters to eat fattening and unhealthy snacks, such as sweets, soft drinks and salty chips.

Overweight people are physically less active. How unfortunate! Continued physical activity in adulthood—whether competitive or non-competitive—can be a major and readily available contributor to healthy self-esteem.

It doesn't take a rocket scientist to figure out what needs to be done here. TV limitations are necessary, but they must be clearly understood and routine policy around the house. The wars will be unending if Mom and Dad attempt to implement a hit-or-miss approach.

5. Transitions

A lot of transitions that occur while children grow up are difficult, but perhaps the hardest—as we have seen before—is the move into junior high. Research indicates that when a lot of changes occur simultaneously, self-esteem and self-confidence may suffer. During the move into junior high, children are experiencing several changes:

1. The move from a small school to a larger, more impersonal one.
2. The introduction of the dimension of romantic appeal into the self-esteem equation.
3. The beginning of dating relationships.
4. The emotional and physical changes of puberty.

It is especially important during this time that parents realize their children need more—not less—support and guidance. Many parents hear only the "Stay out of my life!" message that comes with the beginning of adolescence. The kids want to be more on their own, it seems,which hurts the feelings of many parents, who then pull away even more.

On the contrary, what is needed with preadolescents and early adolescents is a good dose of the basic self-esteem strategies we have just described. Shared fun on a regular basis and active, sympathetic listening are very helpful, and do not have to offend the child's growing sense of independence. Positive reinforcement can also help young teens know when they are on track and doing a good job.

What doesn't help? Nagging, lectures, arguing and impromptu discussions about problems. The hard part about being the parent of adolescents is finding the right combination of limit-setting and letting go, as well as the ability to tolerate nonessential differences. *Surviving Your Adolescents* provides specific suggestions for practicing the difficult art of "raising" teens.

6. Effort and Courage

Next on our most overlooked list are two aspects of character. Are expending effort and taking risks becoming lost arts? The situation is probably not that bad, but it does seem that effort and courage have somehow become more disconnected from self-esteem. They have become separated from the Great Evaluator. People seem to admire these qualities in others, but not in themselves.

What a shame! People who are willing to use more elbow grease and who are willing to face up to anxious situations are, in general, going to be more successful and thus feel better about themselves. If you want to start and succeed at your own business some day, for example, you'll need plenty of guts and effort. If you want to maintain your good friends or have your marriage succeed, you'd better be capable of self-sacrifice as well as willing to face the anxiety of bringing up and discussing unpleasant subjects.

These facts may seem obvious, but in our society today they are often disregarded. We have become too focused on ability and *not focused enough on how to push ourselves*. We treat competition like a four-letter word, rather than as possible motivation to do better. We feel anyone should be entitled to anything simply because they're here and he wants it.

We may think whatever we want, but the real world will always run a lot on guts and effort. If your children appreciate this reality, chances are they will be successful in life and feel good about themselves. You want them to appreciate both their efforts and their accomplishments. How you play the game—and how the game turns out—are both important.

How do you get your children to feel proud of themselves for their effort and courage? A couple of tips may be helpful. You don't lecture or nag them into feeling this way. Instead, you praise them when they behave with character and you model it yourself.

7. Facing Problems Squarely

"I'm so worried about my Bobby. I've felt there's been something wrong ever since he was little." I've heard statements like this many times over twenty-five years of practicing psychology, and they always make me irritated. Such remarks make no sense.

Instead of screaming, though, I always ask politely, "If you were feeling concerned, what prevented you from getting an evaluation to

determine if there was a problem or not?" The answers have been many.
"We couldn't afford it." "I was afraid it would lower his self-esteem by
taking him to a shrink." "My husband was against the idea." "I thought
maybe the problem would go away."

Meanwhile, Bobby grew up with an undiagnosed learning disability,
Attention Deficit Disorder, undue anxiety or some other problem. Now
Bobby's sixteen and the damage to his life and his self-esteem is severe
and perhaps irreparable.

*Parents' "intuition," especially that of mothers, is usually very
accurate.* If you suspect a problem, look into it immediately. If you are
proven correct, then you can do something about it. If you are wrong, then
you can relax.

The only thing you can hurt by waiting is your child's self-esteem.

16

Managing Self-Prejudice in Children

M arci brings home her report card, which consists of all As and one A-minus. In spite of the excitement and praise of her parents, she seems unhappy with her performance and mopes around the whole evening. Finally, Mom can't stand it anymore and breaks the ice:

"What's the matter, honey? You look like you just lost you last friend?"

"My report card stinks!"

"How can you say that? It was wonderful."

"Maybe to you, but I could—and should—have gotten straight As. That A-minus in history was not necessary. Mrs. Benko is unfair a lot of times, but I should have thought of that and studied harder."

"I thought you studied quite hard."

"But I should have done more! That's the point. I'm never going to get into a good college if I keep being lazy and babying myself all the time."

"Now, dear, you know that's not the case. Why..."

> "IT IS THE CASE, MOM! Don't you start trying to be
> nice to me just because you're my mother! The
> competition out their is fierce to the max!"

As we saw in the chapter on self-doubt, children's self-esteem can suffer when they accurately see a problem or weakness in themselves. They can also suffer lowered self-esteem when they misperceive their strengths or weaknesses. Marci's trouble is an example of *self-prejudice*. Marci maintains a negative belief about herself in spite of contrary evidence.

We don't totally understand why kids think this way, but we do know that some are more prone to it than others. We can identify several different causes of self-prejudice:

1. Repeated, inaccurate messages from adults have been "internalized" by the Great Evaluator
2. Perfectionistic standards
3. Anxiety and/or depression
4. "Key competitor" problems

Inaccurate Messages from Adults

Certainly self-prejudice can occur when the Evaluator in a child has picked up from adults strong or repeated negative messages that are themselves inaccurate. The Great Evaluator is not always real bright, and he assumes that if important people say something enough times, it must be correct.

> "You'll never amount to anything."
> "Can't you listen to me for once in your life?"
> "How about showing just a little respect for a change?"
> "Keep eating like that you'll be a blimp in no time."
> "Why are you always so rude to your friends?"
> "It just seems we can't ever trust you at all."

Unless the child being referred to in these comments is a total loss to humanity, these remarks probably reflect more on the amount of adult upset than on the severity of the child's infraction. People who make comments like this often operate according to the old law: "Angry people speak, happy ones remain silent." The criticisms are overdone. Notice all the extreme words, such as "never," "ever," "for once" and "always." Because the parent is very upset, the child is being portrayed as a scoundrel. Repeat this enough times to a youngster and her Evaluator will become the Critical Tyrant.

Perfectionistic Standards

Just like Marci, many children develop perfectionistic standards for themselves. They feel the only satisfactory performance is a perfect one. When they are trying to achieve something, *there are really only two possibilities: perfection or failure*. Since perfection is usually impossible to attain, the person will continually be criticizing herself.

Certainly, some perfectionistic standards can be taught to children by their parents or other adults. I remember the case of one father who would review his twelve-year-old son's homework each night. If it wasn't done perfectly, the father would tear it up and make the boy start over. What a way to spend the evening!

Other kids seem to develop perfectionistic ideas for reasons we don't really understand. For some of these children, the stress they put on themselves results in tremendous achievements, but they still maintain their self-prejudice and, sadly, can't appreciate what they have accomplished. The Great Evaluator says "Not good enough," instead of the more realistic, "Good job—you put a lot of work into that!"

Anxiety and/or Depression

Children who tend to be anxious or depressed are also likely to be self-critical, even in the face of their obvious successes. Anxious kids may enjoy an accomplishment for a short period of time. Then, however, they may feel that whatever they have accomplished in the past is likely to be unrepeatable in the future. They always seem to have to find something to worry about. Even though they may have really succeeded, they think their "luck" is going to run out and a crash is inevitable.

Depressed children, on the other hand, often are unable to appreciate anything they do. Like those who have been abused, their successes don't ring a bell with their Great Evaluator. They remain bland about the whole thing and don't voice much self-confidence, but they may be quick to recognize or admit to faults.

For some children both anxiety and depression seem to regularly attack their self-esteem. Mack is worried that Judy will reject him when he asks her for a date. He asks her anyway. (This takes a lot of guts, which he doesn't give himself credit for at all.) He is shocked when she says "Yes, I'd love to." Now after the phone call, he is feeling depressed because he is sure she'll think he's a dork and he's thinking what an idiot he was for getting himself into this mess in the first place. This is vintage, Grade-A Self-Prejudice!

"Key Competitor" Problems

Some children develop self-prejudice and problems with poor self-esteem because they are obsessed with comparing themselves to one or two specific people. Not surprisingly, these people may often be close to them. They may be their best friends, or same-sex siblings.

This kind of competition can be a real strain on youngsters. Instead of emphasizing how he has done compared to himself in the past, or how he is doing compared to an overall reference group, he focuses entirely on doing better than this one person. If I do better than Jack on the math test, my self-esteem soars. But if he does better than I do on the baseball field, I am crushed.

In these situations a realistic sense of success or failure is obliterated by a focus on a very narrowly defined, win-or-lose competition. There are no thoughts like "I did pretty well," or "I need to improve on this or that," or "My effort was really good even though I hated the outcome." It's only "I'm great and wonderful if I beat him, and I am a jerk if I don't."

Unfortunately, when people do this kind of competing, they usually compare themselves to others who are at least as good or better than they are. In a sense, this way of thinking looks like a good strategy for self-improvement. In the long run, however, it produces turmoil and demoralization. Adolescents are especially competitive in this way. The good news, however, is that if contact is broken off with one's Key Competitor (through their moving out of town, for example), that person doesn't have to be replaced. Some kids can settle down and start evaluating themselves more realistically.

How to Manage Self-Prejudice

Dealing with self-prejudicial children is tricky. It's all too easy to get baited into a crazy and confusing conversation that just leaves you frustrated, worried and mad. On the one hand you feel compassionate, and on the other hand you feel irritated. Here are some suggestions.

1. *Are you causing the problem?* Make sure first that you, as a parent, are not the important adult who is giving strong, repeated and inaccurate feedback to your child. Do you only talk when you're angry? Are *you* the perfectionist? Do your critical comments use words like "always" or "never"? Do you spout off when you're enraged, or do you wait to calm down before speaking about something that's bothering you?

Are you the authoritarian type of parent we described earlier? Or are you also regularly capable of building self-esteem through the other strategies we discussed, such as reasonable discipline, listening, positive reinforcement and fun? If you are not doing these things, maybe it's you who is unwittingly converting your child's Great Evaluator into a Critical Tyrant.

On the other hand, perhaps it's someone else in the family, like your spouse, who is providing the inaccurate, negative feedback. Perhaps you'd better bite the bullet and confront him or her. When doing this—even with an adult—keep in mind the rules for giving negative feedback.

Remember that *accurate* negative messages to your child are often necessary and can give a youngster a chance to improve. They must be given in the proper, thoughtful way, however.

2. *Is the child baiting you?* For some crazy reason, many kids love to complain about themselves in front of their parents. For some kids it's a way to torture their parents when the kids are upset about something but can't get mad directly. For others, it may be an indirect way of fishing for compliments. You put yourself down first, then sit back and wait for the praise and emotional support to roll in.

For these children, the problem is not too serious, because they may not really believe their own self-put-downs in the first place. If you think this is the case—that it's just a kind of pastime for them—take it with a grain of salt and don't worry too much about their self-esteem.

3. *Direct contradiction and emotional upset are not useful.* In the example at the beginning of this chapter, Marci was *not* baiting her mother. She was serious. Mom was bewildered, and naturally enough, she made two mistakes:

1. She tried direct contradiction, saying, "I thought you
   studied quite hard," and "Now, dear, you know
   that's not the case. Why..."
2. She started getting upset.

Both of these "tactics" will reinforce a child's perception that her self-criticisms were correct in the first place. Better tactics include the careful use of sympathetic listening and strategy of building a self-concept.

4. *Self-concept building.* Self-prejudice can often be successfully dented or eroded if a parent takes other opportunities to contradict what the child may have been saying about herself. Once Marci got to the point where she was getting irritated with her mother, for example, Mom wasn't going to be able to do much good.

At other times, however, Mom might say things such as:

"I noticed you put a lot of work into that paper."
"I'm more than happy with your academic work."
"I know you may not agree sometimes, but I heard
  your father tell one of his associates the other day
  how pleased he was with your effort in school. He's
  delighted with how you're doing."

In these examples, Mom is careful to keep her comments short and rather low-key. She also does not lecture her daughter about her misperceptions, and she even acknowledges briefly that Marci sometimes entertains a different opinion.

If Marci counters by repeating her own view of her academic prowess, Mom should handle her daughter gently and casually:

> "Right, Mom, that's what you always say."
>
> "I'm not stupid, dear, and I do think I'm correct."
>
> "So you think I'm stupid, is that it?"
>
> "You're probably a lot smarter than I am. It's just you're a little hard on yourself at times."
>
> "That's the only way to get ahead. Laziness pays less than minimum wage."
>
> "Well, you certainly are a hard case. You're far from lazy, and I'm checking out of this conversation for a while. See you later, honey."

A-plus for Mom. Perhaps Marci got the message—a little.

5. *Be careful with active listening.* If you're going to actively listen to a child, and the child is only tearing herself apart, don't you run the risk of reinforcing the very problem you want to help with?

Yes, you do, but you can minimize this risk with a slightly different version of listening. Devin, nine years old, comes home from his baseball game:

> "How was the game?"
>
> "Rotten. We lost and I struck out for the last out."
>
> "Oh no! What a shame."
>
> "I'm an idiot."
>
> "Why do you say that?"
>
> "What do you mean why?! Because I made the last stupid out and we lost."
>
> "So that makes you an idiot, huh?"
>
> "Sure does."
>
> "Let me think for a second. I suppose you made all the other outs for your team as well."
>
> "I couldn't have. You know that."
>
> "Yes I do. But do you think all the other guys who made outs are idiots, too, or is it just you because you made the last one?"
>
> "I made the last one, so I'm an idiot."
>
> "Baseball sounds like a tough game, then, since every

game has to wind up with some poor slob feeling like an idiot."

"Well, how would you feel?"

"Believe it or not, when I was a little girl, I played more baseball than you ever will. And I made plenty of last outs. If you think I enjoyed that, you're nuts, but I never thought I was a complete knucklehead either. Just like you, I did pretty good the rest of the time."

Will the maternal Socrates win the day? She may if she shuts up pretty soon, but it's likely in the meantime that she was successful in toning down her son's self-criticism.

One last caution about dealing with self-prejudice: *make sure it is self-prejudice*. Self-esteem problems based on *accurate* perceptions are an entirely different problem that may require effort to change, and certainly not superficial reassurance.

17

Turning the Switch

We mentioned earlier that good parenting involves providing self-discipline and self-esteem for your children. If you have read *1-2-3 Magic* and/or *Surviving Your Adolescents*, you have good ideas for how to manage the discipline side of things. At this point in this book, you now also have some concrete ideas about how to foster the self-esteem of your children.

How do parents become comfortable switching from the one mode to another? As we said before, although both good discipline and good self-esteem strategies reinforce each other, they by no means come easily and they are often accompanied by opposite emotional states. This internal juggling act is difficult. Discipline may often be accompanied by the feeling of irritation, while the fostering of self-esteem is often accompanied by affection and warmth.

The problem is you have to provide for both discipline and self-esteem, but because kids are inconsistent your feelings change. *You* have to provide the consistency and make sure your efforts are appropriate to the situation. When discipline is required, you set limits. When self-esteem needs a boost, you encourage.

Obviously, your efforts will not always fit your feelings. There are two possibilities:

1. *Parents' feelings fit what is needed* in a situation, e.g., I am irritated over the kids fighting and discipline is required, or I am proud of them and praise would be a good idea.

2. *Parents' feelings do not fit what is needed* in a situation, e.g., I am irritated about my lousy day at work, but affectionate positive reinforcement is appropriate because of an unusual act of kindness by one of my children.

When the Feelings Fit

John comes home from a rotten day at the office, and as he walks in the door he hears the frantic screaming of Johnny, his eight year old, and Bobby, his six-year-old. Dad is now *more crabby* and must count them before his blood boils and he does something stupid. "That's 1 for both you guys," he says. He has given them their first warning.

For the past twenty minutes Mom has been watching her four-year-old daughter carry buckets of water and try to pour them in the bird bath in the back yard. About forty percent of the water has found its way to its proper destination, while the rest is on Tracey's shoes and all over the ground.

Mom is feeling affectionate and proud of her daughter's kindness. She opens the window and calls out, "Tracey, what a good girl! Those thirsty birds are sure going to be happy to get a drink." Tracey beams.

When the Feelings Do Not Fit

Now let's have John come home again from his rotten day at the office. He looks out the window and sees Tracey pouring water partly in the bird bath and partly soaking her gym shoes.

For a few seconds, he's tempted, because of his mood, to see this as the last straw in his day and to yell out the window, "Tracey, put that down now, you're getting it all over yourself." He recovers, however, realizes his daughter is trying to be kind and enjoys watching her intent on doing her thing. She's cute as a button. Later, after he settles down a bit, he'll praise her for her kindness. The shoes will dry. He's made a good emotional switch. He controlled his negative mood, took a deep breath, and allowed himself to appreciate the situation and his daughter's kindness—an important part of character.

Here's another example of good switching, but this time it goes in the opposite direction; affection in the next example must be replaced by discipline. Dad and Tom have just returned home from bowling. They had a great time. Dad was proud of his son's improving ability. He had praised him often, with comments like "Nice shot!," "Good ball!," "That was a tough one to get," and "Your form looks real good." After bowling they went out for their favorite lunch—pizza buffet.

Dad's feeling proud and affectionate, but two minutes after they walk in the door, Tom is engaged in one of his favorite pastimes: teasing the dog. The dog is standing awkwardly on two legs as the boy pins him in the corner. A sinister growl, which Dad has heard before, signals trouble.

"Tom, that's enough." Tom acts as if he doesn't hear. "That's 1," says Dad, giving the first real warning. Tom leaves the dog and runs in the other room. Dad's good switch helps preserve the nice day.

Let's imagine Dad didn't switch in this situation. He thinks, "I know he's making the dog growl and we don't usually let him do that, but he's not likely to get bit and *I hate to ruin our nice day by having to discipline him.*" Dangerous thinking.

Tom continues to harrass the dog. The growling gets worse. Dad says nothing. The dog nips Tom on the cheek. Screaming, Tom slaps the dog in the head and the dog runs away.

Dad yells, "How many times have I told you not to tease that (blank) dog! You keep up this stupid behavior and we're going to have to get rid of him. YOU HEAR ME?!"

The nice day is ruined, and all the good that bowling together did is gone with the wind.

Switching is often very difficult, especially when parents have to manage their own moods, the moods of their spouses, and the changing behavior of their children. It's totally unrealistic, however, to expect the kids to provide the consistency or for them to know what's needed in each situation. Though it may feel at times like mission impossible, you can learn, with practice, to provide alternately for both discipline and self-esteem.

Part V

Where They're Headed

18

Revolutions in Adulthood

F or children self-esteem is a revolutionary business. Its foundations change repeatedly, which requires a lot of adjustment and work. Good self-esteem depends upon adequate success (both earned and unearned) and a fair internal judge—one that is not prone to perfectionism, the exaggeration of weaknesses or the overlooking of strengths.

Self-esteem revolutions continue in adulthood. They are still of immense importance, but they are less frequent. There are more "developmental" tasks to be conquered, and once again self-esteem will depend on the outcome. Though the Great Evaluator may mellow some with age, there is still potential for self-esteem highs and lows.

As parents let their kids go, they hope they have accomplished much. They hope to have helped provide their children with the *social skills* necessary to work and play with other people, and to maintain lasting relationships. They hope to have nurtured in their kids the intellectual skills and abilities necessary for organizing their own affairs, as well as for achieving *competence* in their chosen line of work. They also hope to have fostered in their sons and daughters, for their continuing health and enjoyment, an interest in and respect for their *physical* selves.

Finally, parents hope that *character* and self-esteem have become connected in their children. They want their kids to be able to feel proud of themselves for their hard work, persistence and effort. They want them to take pride in their ability to make adjustments and bounce back after they have failed or received valid, negative feedback. They want them to feel good about themselves when they do something important and worthwhile, even though it may scare them to death. They also want them to be kind and to be concerned about the welfare of other people. These qualities will aid the children later as they struggle with the self-esteem revolutions that occur in adult life.

The Career Revolution

As an adult most everyone must make a choice, at some time or another, about what kind of work she wants to do. The implications of this choice for self-esteem are, of course, profound. Whether or not they want to admit it, people often see different occupations as more desirable or respectable than others. This perception has a lot to do with career choice. Many young men and women, for example, see becoming a doctor or a policeman as jobs that automatically bestow self-respect.

When people want to demean this kind of motivation, they refer to it as "status-seeking." For most people, though, self-esteem and job choice are very much connected one way or another. Certainly for many people pursuing public office the desire for fame and recognition is very much a part of their self-esteem profile.

Yet, career choice is only the beginning. Society may not feel you have the necessary qualities for your chosen line of work. You may not be able to get into medical school or law school, or into training for law enforcement. The shock of this rejection to someone who has had his heart set on a certain, special career is a very jarring self-esteem revolution itself. Now he must go to his second or third choice, and may permanently feel somewhat unfulfilled. This setback will be an early adult test of the capacity to recover from failure.

For those who do begin a career—whether it represents their heart's desire or not—the next major impact on what they think of themselves will come from how they perform on the job. *Except in rare cases, there will be no entitlement here*. Self-esteem will have to be earned, and the young adults' past experiences and resources in the social, competence and character dimensions of their life will play a large role. No one will be around who will think they are "a wonder just the way they are." The interpersonal skills, ability and effort put forth—as well as our old friend, luck—will determine the outcome.

The Marriage Revolution

Most adults will marry or decide to live with someone on a permanent basis. The effects of this decision on self-esteem will be profound, but the difficulty of this enterprise is always terribly underestimated. People enter marriage hopeful, idealistic, inexperienced and naive.

Similar to job choice, young adults often think marriage involves an automatic increase in self-esteem. This perception is really not inaccurate or self-deceptive. Finding a partner who is willing to spend the rest of his or her life with you is a major challenge, and it is certainly something that should make you feel good.

The divorce rates for both first and second marriages in this country, however, still hover around fifty percent. Think of the painful self-esteem crashes divorce—as well as the conflict that preceeds it—causes for millions of men and women.

In addition, marriage itself severely tests the interpersonal skills and character of everyone who enters into it. Spouses go through predictable stages that involve disillusionment, hostility and boredom. When marriage works out well, it can be a major contributor to the self-esteem of an adult.

The greatest compliment you can pay somebody is to want to spend your entire life with them. Unfortunately, the greatest insult is to reverse the decision.

The Parenting Revolution

Eventually most people who marry must also brace themselves for another tumultuous change in their adult lives: parenting. The day that first little one comes home marks a lifestyle revolution that won't be reversed for at least eighteen years. No longer is it just the two of you, and no longer can you go out without getting a sitter or bringing you-know-who along.

Next to diving into marriage, having children may be one of the most poorly planned things adults do. Most young adults are ridiculously unprepared for parenthood and have little idea what they are getting themselves into. How can anyone posssibly know in the first place? Kids can be one of life's biggest delights as well as one of life's biggest aggravations, and they greatly complicate the marriage relationship. The parenting instinct is extremely strong in most people, so both having children and how well their children are doing will affect Mom and Dad's self-esteem considerably.

The parenting revolution affects the self-esteem of women and men differently. In our society, Mom usually takes the brunt of raising the little ones, while Dad continues with his outside job. This arrangement has some advantages, for despite what some men claim, women are very likely much better at the job.

The danger, however, is that Mom's self-esteem may suffer. First of all, while father may get stressed out, his job still involves challenge, contact with other adults, and pay. Mom's, however, involves routine tasks, contact with babbling toddlers and no monetary reward. Second, our society does not respect mothering as it should. For many women their competence as a mother and the effort they expend in that job is important to them, but only weakly connected to their Evaluator. Much as we saw with the issue of character, a lot of hard work does not seem to produce a corresponding improvement in self-esteem.

Many women, of course, are perfectly happy at home. Their mothering does contribute a lot to their self-esteem. Others, however, feel that their piece of the self-esteem pie lies in "working outside the home," which would be fine except they now must, in actual fact, hold down *two full-time jobs*. As many women have pointed out, their self-esteem may now rest on the overwhelming and often perfectionistic task of being Superwoman: perfect mother, perfect wife, perfect homemaker. The effect of all this on self-respect can be brutal.

As their children grow older, parents find that their self-esteem is tied, to some extent, to how well their kids are doing. This connection is a perfectly normal part of the parenting self-esteem revolution. There's certainly nothing abnormal about feeling proud of that little "chip off the old block,"or feeling embarrassed when he goofs up.

Kids are also excellent providers of something else for their parents: play, or "non-self-esteem" time. They are very good at having fun themselves, and can help Mom and Dad relive their own childhoods as well as get back to enjoying the present.

Humility, Compassion and Self-Acceptance

As time goes on, adulthood usually brings other changes in self-esteem. You have to deal with changes in health and overall physical condition. Self-esteem can also take something of a beating with the arrival of age thirty, age forty and age fifty. Other idiosyncratic self-esteem revolutions, such as unemployment or job changes, the addition or loss of friends or relatives, and geographical moves also have effects.

On the other hand, as people grow older many find the push for self-esteem becomes less urgent. They have grown up, and have successfully accomplished most of the jobs life has given them. The Great Evaluator has done his job and now is mellowing. Self-esteem still exists, but with time men and women often become more able to look at themselves—and life—in a more mature, realistic way.

This point of view often involves the development of humility, compassion and self-acceptance. You might say humility is the realistic appreciation of the role of *good luck* in one's life. A person begins to realize that, although what she accomplished and enjoyed was partly a result of her own efforts, it was also due to the resources she happened to be blessed with and to the efforts of other people. In other words, humility means she can feel proud of herself, but take her success with a few grains of salt.

Compassion, on the other hand, might be described as the realistic appreciation of the role of *bad luck* in someone's life—either one's own or someone else's. An individual begins to appreciate that his shortcomings and mistakes were to a large extent his own doing, but, then again, life threw him a few unexpected curves along the way. Perhaps he did the best he could.

Together, realistic humility and compassion can generate a down-to-earth self-acceptance as one grows older. Self-acceptance is not the same as self-esteem, because different people with varying levels of self-esteem—with the aid of humility and compassion—may still be able to accept themselves for the most part. Except where self-esteem is consistently very low, many people learn to say, "These are my good points and these are my weaknesses. I'm doing about as well as I can, considering all the circumstances, and I'm enjoying life most of the time."

Humility, compassion, appreciation of one's own efforts, and enjoyment of the results. Perhaps this is the recipe for a mature combination of adequate self-esteem and sensible self-acceptance.

This state of mind, however, is for adults only. Though it may sound funny, you wouldn't want your children to accept themselves the way they are. They have a job to do, and that's growing up. For our youngsters, luck, hard work, and the Great Evaluator will always be necessary parts of the struggle for self-esteem.

Bibliography

Baumrind, Diana. Authoritarian vs. authoritative parental control. *Adolescence*, 3, 255-272, 1963.

Baumrind, Diana. Some thoughts about childrearing. In U. Bronfenbrenner & M. Mahoney (Eds.), *Influences on Human Development*. Hinsdale, Illinois: Dryden Press, 1975.

Bednar, Richard & Peterson, Scott. *Self-Esteem: Paradoxes and Innovations in Clinical Theory and Practice*. Washington, D.C.: American Psychological Association, 1995.

Berk, Laura E. *Infants, Children, and Adolescents*. Boston: Allyn and Bacon, 1993.

Brandon, Nathaniel. *The Power of Self-Esteem*. Deerfield Beach, Florida: Health Communications, Inc., 1992.

Briggs, Dorothy Corkille. *Your Child's Self-Esteem*. New York: Doubleday, 1970.

Cooley, C.H. *Human Nature and the Social Order*. New York: Scribner's, 1902.

Coopersmith, Stanley. *The Antecedents of Self-Esteem*. San Francisco: W.H. Freeman, 1967.

Covington, M.V. and Beery, R.G. *Self-Worth and School Learning.* New York: Holt, Rinehart, & Winston, 1976.

Damon, William. *Greater Expectations: Overcoming the Culture of Indulgence in America's Homes and Schools.* New York: The Free Press, 1995.

Ellis, Albert & Harper, Robert. *A New Guide to Rational Living.* North Hollywood, California: Wilshire Book Company, 1975.

Deci, Edwards L. and Ryan, Richard M. Human autonomy: the basis for true self-esteem. In Kernis, Michael H. (Ed.) *Efficacy, Agency, and Self-Esteem.* New York: Plenum Press, 1995.

Dyer, Wayne. *Pulling Your Own Strings.* New York: Avon Books, 1977.

Forward, Susan. *Toxic Parents.* New York: Bantam Books, 1989.

Ginott, Haim G. *Between Parent and Child.* New York: Macmillan Co., 1965.

Ginott, Haim G. *Between Parent and Teenager.* New York: Macmillan Co., 1969.

Glasser, William. *Schools without Failure.* New York: Harper & Row, 1969.

James, William. *Principles of Psychology.* New York: Holt, 1890.

Kernis, Michael H. (Ed.) *Efficacy, Agency, and Self-Esteem.* New York: Plenum Press, 1995.

Leo, John. The trouble with self-esteem. *U.S. News & World Report,* April 2, 1990.

Markus, H. and Wurf, E. The dynamic self-concept: a social psychological perspective. In M.R. Rosenzweig & L.W. Porter (Eds.), *Annual Review of Psychology,* 38, 299-337, 1987.

McKay, Matthew & Fanning, Patrick. *Self-Esteem.* New York: St. Martin's Paperbacks, 1987.

Mead, George H. *Mind, Self, and Society.* Chicago: University of Chicago Press, 1934.

May, R. *The Discovery of Being.* New York: Norton, 1983.

Owens, Karen. *Raising Your Child's Inner Self-Esteem.* New York: Plenum Press, 1995.

Payne, Lauren Murphy. *Just Because I Am: A Child's Book of Affirmation.* Minneapolis: Free Spirit Publishing, 1994.

Phelan, Thomas W. *1-2-3 Magic: Effective Discipline for Children 2-12*. Glen Ellyn, Illinois: Child Management, Inc., 1995.

Phelan, Thomas W. *Surviving Your Adolescents*. Glen Ellyn, Illinois: Child Management, Inc., 1994.

Rice, F. Philip. *The Adolescent: Development, Relationships and Culture*. Boston: Allyn and Bacon, 1993.

Rosenberg, M. *Conceiving the Self*. New York: Basic Books, 1979.

Seligman, D. Baby talk. *Fortune*, February 26, 1990.

Seligman, Martin E. *What You Can Change... And What You Can't*. New York: Fawcett Columbine, 1993.

Sykes, Charles. *Dumbing Down Our Kids*. New York: St. Martin's Press, 1995.